THE *Airliner World* BOOK OF THE
BOEING 747

MARK NICHOLLS

KEY BOOKS

Key Books Ltd
PO Box 100, Stamford, Lincolnshire PE9 1XQ
United Kingdom

Telephone: +44 (0) 1780 755131
E-mail: keybooks@keypublishing.com

First published in Great Britain by
Key Books Ltd in 2002

ISBN 0-946219-61-3

British Library Cataloguing in Publication Data:
A catalogue record for this book is available from
the British Library

Designed by DAG Publications Ltd
Printed in Spain by Book Print

Above: Israeli flag carrier El Al has rationalised
its fleet in recent months in response to the
continuing problems within its borders which
has caused a drop in international air travel. It
still operates the 747, a -400 series being shown
here. (*Airliner World* collection)

A Singapore Airlines 747-400 soars into the air on another long haul flight. (*Airliner World* collection)

CONTENTS

① INTRODUCTION

Ask anyone to name a modern commercial airliner and the chances are they will come up with the Concorde or the Jumbo Jet. Why the Jumbo Jet? In a word – size. When it entered commercial aviation service in 1970, the Boeing 747 Jumbo Jet was the largest airliner ever built, being more than twice the size of previous designs. For 30 years it has retained this title, and will not surrender it to the new Airbus A380 until 2006. It has been developed through a series of variants, sold to dozens of airlines and is still in production. It introduced new levels of passenger comfort and amenities, and brought with it an even higher level of in-built safety features. During the past three decades, 747s have carried millions of people for millions of miles and revolutionised air travel almost beyond measure.

It was during the 1960s that it became evident that air travel was a booming business and that extra capacity was urgently needed. Juan Trippe, boss of Pan American Airways, saw the potential for the new aircraft and on April 12, 1966, he signed contracts with Boeing's President, Bill Allen, for 25 Boeing 747s with a value of $550 million – the largest value airliner order up to that date.

The effect of this upon the rest of the world's airlines was pronounced and most had to follow suit in order to compete on the lucrative international routes. It was long distance travel in particular that the 747 was designed for – its ability to carry up to 400 passengers over intercontinental distances, at a higher cruising speed than before and at lower cost per seat mile, made the type an instant winner with both airlines and passengers.

However, Boeing originally proposed the aircraft to fulfil a US Air Force requirement for a large strategic airlifter during a competition in the early 1960s. The new and very large strategic airlifter had to be capable of carrying up to 750 troops or 125,000lb (56,700kg) of cargo for up to 8,000 miles (12,872km). Lockheed won this contract with its C-5 Galaxy but Boeing saw mileage in pursuing the concept and modifying its design for the commercial market. From the very outset, the aircraft was designed as a cargo carrier because at the time it was envisaged that supersonic passenger aircraft would rule the skies from about 1980, and the 747 would be relegated solely to cargo use. History has proven this not to be the case, but the cargo factor had great bearing on the final layout of the aircraft and its commercial success.

A single deck wide-body fuselage was settled upon that could accommodate two rows of 8ft (2.4m) wide standard cargo containers side-by-side, loaded through an upward-hinging nose door. When adapted to carry passengers, the vast cabin had room for twin aisles, galley areas and other amenities, while still affording room for up to 400 passengers and freight in the lower holds. The requirement for front loading access meant that the cockpit was raised and a second deck added to the front of the aircraft – the streamlined taper resulting in the classic 747 humped shape.

Above all, Boeing had to ensure that the aircraft was as safe as possible; it had to be because it would be carrying such large numbers of passengers. As a result, Joe Sutter, head of the 747 design team, insisted on an incredible amount of safety features being built into the aircraft. It

Right: A Swissair 747-357 approaches the gate at Zurich, clearly demonstrating the amount of room required to accommodate one of these huge aircraft. (Chris Penney)

Lower right: One of most famous approaches in commercial aviation was that to Hong Kong's Kai Tak airport. Here Cathay Pacific 747-267B VR-HIB comes in over the crowded city on November 17, 1994. (Robbie Shaw)

Below: The cockpit of a 747-200 series 'classic' operated by Virgin Atlantic Airways in July 2000. With the arrival of the -400 series the Flight Engineers position as well as hundreds of dials and switches were eliminated. (KEY - Chris Penney)

had quadruple redundancy, in other words four hydraulic systems each driven by a different engine, three wing spars for tremendous strength, split control surfaces ensuring that a back-up was always available and an emergency landing gear extension system. The fuel system was equally complex, yet was designed to maintain fuel feed to the engines through a series of pump and pressure feed back-up systems.

Pan Am put its aircraft into revenue earning service from January 1970 and, with other airlines quick to follow, the world of commercial air travel was changed forever. The aircraft's capacity for passengers and freight produced up to 30% per seat mile savings over the older Boeing 707. Therefore, as well as the obvious cost benefits to the airlines, it was also possible to offer cheaper tickets to passengers, thus opening up the world of international travel to many more people.

During its career so far, the 747 has evolved through a series of variants and is still the subject of further development. Each of these variants is dealt with in the subsequent chapters of this book, the aim of which is to illustrate the story of one of the most significant aircraft in aviation history.

The world of commercial aviation was dealt a severe and tragic blow on September 11, 2001, when terrorists hijacked four airliners in the USA and crashed three of them into high value targets, the World Trade Centre in New York and the Pentagon in Washington DC. The consequent effects on commercial air travel were immediate and substantial. Airlines around the world, but in particular those flying to the USA, suffered a drop in bookings and this could not have come at a worse time. The industry was already in a trough, with over capacity already requiring cutbacks, but this has been exacerbated considerably in the months after the attacks. Airlines have rationalised their fleets with older aircraft, including many 747-200 series classics being put into storage. Most will remain there and never re-enter service and similarly a number of well known airlines are also facing extinction. On November 7, 2001, the Belgian national carrier Sabena filed for bankruptcy and at the time a number of other airlines were also considered candidates for liquidation. One of the long-term effects is likely to be a consolidation among European airlines, in a similar fashion to that which has already happened in the USA, with many national carriers disappearing for good.

This book has been produced by Key Books, a division of Key Publishing, one of the world's leading aviation magazine publishers. Included in its portfolio is Airliner World, a monthly magazine that regularly contains news updates and features on the Boeing 747, all Boeing products and indeed anything connected to the commercial aviation industry. More information can be found at its web site: www.airlinerworld.com.

Commercial 747 production	
747-100 series (inc SRs)	205
747-200 series	393
747SP	45
747-300 series	81
747-400 series	569*
Total	1279
* By February 2002 – deliveries continue.	

Above: Boeing 747-123 N9675 (c/n 20390) was converted to a freighter early in its career while still with American Airlines. United Parcels Service (UPS) purchased the aircraft in September 1984, it is now registered N675UP and is still in use – though it is one of a diminishing number of airworthy -100 series. (UPS)

Left: The global appeal of the 747 is epitomised by this image of a United Airlines 747-123 N157UA on approach to Osaka Kansai airport, Japan, in April 1998. The 747 has seen extensive sales to Asian customers, while hundreds more from other operators visit the region every day. (Robbie Shaw)

Left: British Airways is the largest operator of the latest 747 variant, the -400. Boeing announced the launch of the -400 series in 1985 and it has proved to be the most popular version with over 600 ordered so far. (Rich Hunt)

The road that led to the first flight of the 747 prototype on February 9, 1969, may have been rocky, but at least it was short. As Boeing put the data gleaned from the Strategic Airlifter to use on the commercial project, Pan American World Airways became interested and issued a letter of intent to purchase the new Boeing in December 1965. The risks for the Boeing Company were enormous – had the project failed, the company would almost certainly have gone bust.

More than 50 different designs were studied, including one for a double deck, though this was dropped because problems were envisaged over cargo loading, passenger evacuation and servicing of the aircraft. Eventually a wide body was settled upon but the team of designers and engineers still had a huge job ahead of them. This was aviation engineering on an unparalleled scale and it had to be achieved in the shortest time ever for a modern airliner, a feat that remains unchallenged to this day.

Indeed the first aircraft, registration N7470, was not technically an official prototype but built to the standard 747-100 specification. When Pan Am committed itself to a 25-aircraft order on April 12, 1966, it set in motion a series of events that even today stretch the imagination.

The first aircraft were to be delivered to the customer in 1969, so in just three years the design had to be finalised, a whole new assembly plant constructed and the first aircraft built, flight tested and certified. Yet despite all of this, Boeing succeeded and following its historic maiden flight, the original 747 undertook a series of test and certification flights, gradually being joined by the early production aircraft.

Once the flight test schedule was underway, it became apparent that the 747 was a relatively easy aircraft to fly and that very few technical problems needed to be overcome. One in particular was a wing flutter problem but this was cured by modifications to the fuel distribution system to maintain better weight balance in the wing tanks. Greatest concern was with the new Pratt & Whitney JT9D turbofan engines. Throughout the flight test programme, some 87 engine breakdowns necessitated 55 engine changes. These new engines were the most powerful to have been fitted to an airliner at the time but following extensive work by the manufacturer, the problems were gradually overcome and the 747 was cleared for passenger service with the issue of full FAA type approval on December 31, 1969.

Below: N7470, the very first Boeing model 747 reflects the early morning sunlight prior to its next test flight. (Boeing)

Above left: Monday, September 30, 1968, and the prototype 747 is rolled out of the massive Everett assembly building before an audience of Boeing employees, airline representatives and VIPs. (Boeing)

Above: N7470 was finished in a white and silver scheme with a red band along the window line. On its roll-out the aircraft was adorned with the insignia of all the customer airlines, which at the time numbered 26. (Boeing)

Upper left: Construction of the prototype began at Everett before the assembly plant was even finished. Here the aircraft awaits the fitting of its four Pratt & Whitney JT9Ds. (Boeing)

Left: The aircraft was 'christened' by stewardesses from all of the 26 customer airlines during the roll-out ceremony. (Boeing)

Left: History is made on February 9, 1969, as N7470 breaks ground for the first time – with Chief Test Pilot Jack Waddell at the controls, Boeing's greatest gamble finally makes it into the air. (Boeing)

Right: During the early flights, the 747 was often accompanied by the Boeing F-86 chase plane. N7470 made its second flight on February 15, 1969, and on this occasion both the flaps and undercarriage were fully retracted. (Boeing)

Right: It was immediately apparent to the flight test crew that the 747 was a very stable aircraft and one that was easy to fly. These impressions helped to dispel fears that such a huge aircraft would be too difficult for most pilots to fly, indeed it has earned the reputation of being a very forgiving aircraft, and is much loved by all those who have flown it. (Boeing)

Right: In 1990 Boeing presented the prototype 747 to the Seattle Museum of Flight. However, since then it has been used for a number of engine development programmes including the flight testing of the Rolls-Royce Trent 800 series in 1995, this engine then being cleared for use aboard the Boeing 777. (Rolls-Royce)

Right: By October 2000 N7470 was firmly on the ground at Boeing Field with its engines detached. Its future with the Seattle Museum of Flight is assured, but the possibility of further flight testing for systems and engine development cannot be ruled out. (Key Publishing – Tony Dixon)

747-100

On its introduction, the 747-100 ushered in a new era of mass transit capability within the airline industry. First to receive the aircraft was the launch customer Pan Am, which took delivery of N733PA *Clipper Young America* on December 12, 1969. The inaugural revenue-earning passenger flight eventually departed Washington Dulles International Airport in the early hours of January 22, 1970, bound for London Heathrow.

Other customers began to receive their aircraft as Boeing ramped up production to a peak of seven aircraft per month in March 1970 and it was not long before many of the world's larger airlines were operating the 747-100 on long-haul flights. Although the new aircraft was cheaper to operate overall, it did require considerable initial investment by both operators and airports. Suddenly airports had to deal with servicing a much bigger aircraft with more catering needs, more fuel, in fact more of everything. Spares provision had to be increased, not only in the number of line items held but also in their considerable sizes. Airport infrastructure had to cope with an increase in the amount of passenger baggage – as much as 85,000lb (38,500kg) of it per aircraft. Other areas affected by the arrival of the 747 were aircraft maintenance and stand/pier space at airports. But although these requirements needed to be addressed, the potential of the aircraft meant it saw little resistance to change. The aircraft also brought with it considerable improvements to passenger comfort, with in-flight movies, a vast airy cabin space and a bar in the First/Business Class lounge area. A happy and contented travelling public means higher customer retention and repeat journeys, thus increasing business for both airlines and airports.

Weight is the enemy of aircraft designers, the heavier the aircraft, the less revenue-earning payload it can carry. The 747-100 was originally to have a maximum take-off weight of 680,000lb (308,448kg) but this grew to 710,000lb (322,056kg) and eventually 735,000lb (333,000kg). This required an increase in engine power, eventually achieved at considerable cost by Pratt & Whitney as the initial teething problems with the new JT9D turbofans were solved.

In all, 167 standard 747-100s were delivered by July 12, 1976, although even before the aircraft's first flight in 1969 Boeing had been studying ideas to increase the all-up weight of the 747 and its payload capacity. As an interim measure Boeing introduced more powerful water-injected JT9D-3AW engines rated at 45,000lb (200.16kN) and made some revisions to the landing gear, flaps, doors and fuel system. This led to what was known as the 747-100A, and a number of airlines returned their original aircraft to receive these modifications. The upgraded aircraft had an increased take-off weight of 755,000lb

747-100 SPECIFICATIONS

Wingspan	195ft 8in (59.6m)
Length	231ft 4in (70.5m)
Height	63ft 5in (19.47m)
Wing area	5,500sq ft (511m²)
Weight empty (min)	348,816lb (158,223kg)
Weight maximum	735,000lb (333,000kg)
Fuel capacity	47,210 – 53,160 US gal (178,690 – 201,210 litres)
Cruising speed	604mph (972km/h)
Ceiling	45,000ft (13,700m)
Range	5,527 miles (8,893km)
Passenger capacity	374-490 (max 516)
Powerplants	choice of: 4 x Pratt & Whitney JT9D-3 4 x General Electric CF6-50E 4 x Rolls-Royce RB211-534B

Right: Trans World Airlines (TWA) was one of the early customers for the 747-100. Here 747-131 N93107 (c/n 19673), the 35th 747 built, gets airborne from London Gatwick for another transatlantic flight. This aircraft was delivered to the airline on April 29, 1970, and spent most of its career with the carrier until it was withdrawn from use in October 1997 and broken up in 1999. (Robbie Shaw)

(342,470kg), which delivered either a 15% increase in payload or a further 460 miles (740km) of range.

Boeing also offered the 747-100B from September 1977, which could be fitted with engines from any of the three major engine manufacturers. Only nine were built, a single JT9D-7F powered aircraft for Iran Air and eight with Rolls-Royce RB211s for Saudi Arabian Airlines. A total of 28 strengthened SR versions of the -100B were built for the domestic Japanese market (see later). Over 90 different operators have flown the 747-100, but today very few -100s remain in service, indeed those that do are for the most part confined to cargo duties. Many of these have either been converted to the SCD (Side Cargo Door) or F (Freighter) configuration.

747–100 OPERATORS

Aer Lingus	Delta Air Lines	NorthWest (Orient) Airlines
Aeroposta	Dominicana	Okada Air
Air Algerie	Eastern Air Lines	Orion Air
Air Atlanta Icelandic	Egypt Air	Overseas National
Air Canada	El Al	Pakistan International Airlines
Air Club International	Evergreen International Airlines	Pan American World Airways
Air Dabia	Federal Express	People Express Airlines
Air Europe	Flying Tiger Line	Polar Air Cargo
Air France	Garuda Indonesian Airways	Qantas
Air Gulf Falcon	Global International Airways	Royal Air Maroc
Air Hong Kong	Iberia	Sabena
Air Jamaica	Icelandair	Saha Airlines
Air Pacific	(Imperial) Iranian Air Force	Saudi Arabian Airlines nee Saudia
Air Zaire	Iran Air	Scanair
Airtours International Airways	Jalways	Scandinavian Airlines System
Alitalia	Japan Air Charter	Southern Air Transport
American Airlines	Japan Air Lines	Tower Air
American International Airways	Japan Asia Airways	Trans Mediterranean Airways
Atlas Air	Kabo Air	Trans World Airlines
Avianca	Kalitta Air	Transamerica Airlines
Braniff Airways	Kitty Hawk International	Tunis Air
Britannia Airways	Lan Chile	United Air Lines
British Airways	Lion Air	United Parcel Service
British Caledonian Airways	Lufthansa	Viasa
Canadian Airlines International	Malaysian Airline System	Virgin Atlantic Airways
Cargo Air Lines	Metro International Airways	Wardair Canada
Cargolux	Middle East Airlines	World Airways
Caribbean Airways	Monarch Airlines	Zambia Airways
China Airlines	NASA	
Continental Airlines	Nationair	Note: Alaska Airlines and Western Air Lines
Corsair	National Airlines	ordered aircraft but these were subsequently
Corse Air International	Nigeria Airways	cancelled.

Left: Boeing 747-132 VR-HKN (c/n 19897) on finals at London Heathrow. Operated by Air Hong Kong it was originally delivered to Delta Airlines on October 22, 1970, and also served with Flying Tiger Line, El Al and FedEx. Its last user was Polar Air Cargo before it was withdrawn from use and stored at Marana, Arizona, from September 1999. (David Stephens Collection)

Left: This 747-133, CF-TOA (c/n 20013), is typical of many -100 series Jumbos. It joined Air Canada on December 8, 1971, and after 12 years with that company was leased to Global International Airways in June 1983. This shot is noteworthy as the aircraft was only with Global until October 3, 1983, when it was returned to Air Canada. From 1984 until 1995 it was passed between a host of operators, eventually being retired and scrapped in October 1995. (Chris Penney)

Left: German carrier Lufthansa was the first international customer for the 747. Its first aircraft, 747-130 D-ABYA (c/n 19746), is seen here on a pre-delivery test flight wearing the registration N1800B. Lufthansa disposed of the aircraft to the ITEL Corporation on November 29, 1978, which leased it to Braniff International. After a number of other leasing companies and operators, it eventually joined Tower Air, which used the aircraft as N603FF. (Boeing)

Right: Operating in what appears to be just an undercoat paint scheme, 747-143 N357AS (c/n 19730) was utilised by Overseas National Airways for a three-month period from July to October in 1983. This small airline also used a few 747-200s at around the same time. This particular aircraft was first operated by Alitalia – it later joined SAS and was subsequently leased to a number of operators prior to being broken up in the late 1990s. (Chris Penney)

Right: Another European operator to make early use of the 747 was Air France. F-BPVD (c/n 19752) was delivered to the airline on July 14, 1970, and apart from a few leasing periods to Nationair, Corsair and Middle East Airlines, it served with the French carrier until January 1994. It was purchased by AAR Aviation Trading as N612AR on January 4, 1994, and then by Tower Air on February 17 of the same year. It was later ferried to Oklahoma City and cannibalised for spares. (Chris Penney)

Lower right: This 747-124 has a most interesting history. It was delivered as N26863 (c/n 19735) to Continental Airlines on August 12, 1970. However, in January 1974 it was withdrawn from use and stored before being re-purchased by Boeing in October 1975. The company converted it to a freighter and it was then bought by the Imperial Iranian Air Force in November 1975. Boeing then re-acquired the aircraft in April 1977 and sold it to Israeli carrier El Al in June that year. In 1981 it was leased by Avianca before being returned to El Al. Here it is seen wearing its Israeli registration 4X-AXZ but retaining the Avianca livery. The aircraft was finally retired in March 1999. (Chris Penney)

Left: Polar Air Cargo took charge of this 747-122F in May 1994 and had it re-registered as N854FT (c/n 19754) on February 9, 1995. It was originally delivered to United Air Lines on August 4, 1970, and from 1985 passed through a number of owner's, including Pan Am. It was also converted twice, once to SCD specification in 1988 and then to a full freighter configuration in 1994. (Robbie Shaw)

Left: Spanish carrier Iberia leased this 747-133, EC-DXE (c/n 20014), from Guinness Peat Aviation in May 1985 for a six-month period. The aircraft's first owner was Air Canada, which took delivery of it on March 18, 1971. It has since had numerous owners, as well as periods of storage. Its last owner was Air Atlanta Icelandic, which also sub-leased it to Saudi Arabian Airlines in February 1999. (Chris Penney)

Left: One of only nine 747-100B specification aircraft built is this 747-168B of Saudia, which the airline took charge of as HZ-AIA on April 24, 1981. Saudia, later Saudi Arabian Airlines, bought eight of the Rolls-Royce BR211 powered aircraft, the only other example went to Iran Air. The -100B featured a reinforced structure and an increased gross weight of 753,000lb (341,560kg), and many of the same features that are available on the 747-200. (Chris Penney)

Right: Another early recipient of the 747 was Japan Air Lines, which has operated many examples of the type since the delivery of this, its first aircraft, on April 22, 1970. JA8101 (c/n 19725) was the 31st 747 off the Everett production line and it continued to serve the airline until August 1992 when it was sold to American International Airways as N701CK. Following conversion to a freighter in October 1992, it flew for four more years until being stored at Oscoda, Michigan, from October 1996. (Chris Penney)

Right: Evergreen International Airlines is one of a number of cargo operators that utilises the prodigious payload capacity of the 747. Illustrated is N481EV (c/n 19896) which was originally delivered to Delta Air Lines as N9896 on September 26, 1970. This aircraft also served with China Airlines, Pan Am and Aerolineas Argentinas during its career and is still current with Evergreen, having been converted to a freighter in 1991. (Airliner World Collection)

Right: N9666 (c/n 20105) was the 77th 747 built and was delivered to American Airlines on October 2, 1970, as a 747-123. Citicorp Industrial Credit Inc purchased the aircraft in March 1984 and leased it to a number of operators, including National Airlines, from June until September 1984. It was eventually bought by United Airlines in January 1988, though it has now been withdrawn from use. (Chris Penney)

Above: NASA has operated two 747s. The first was this example, former American Airlines N9668 (c/n 20107) that was registered to NASA as N905NA in July 1974. Here the aircraft is performing wake vortex experiments prior to its conversion into a Space Shuttle carrier (NASA)

Below: Former Continental Airlines 747-124 N26864 was only used by the airline for three years between 1971-74 before it was temporarily withdrawn from use. Wardair Canada bought the aircraft in December 1974 and registered it as C-FFUN. It was eventually sold to Citibank Canada in September 1988 and was then leased and sub leased to a variety of operators and also saw several periods of storage. It was eventually withdrawn from use in June 1997 and stored at Marana, Arizona. (Chris Penney)

Above: N659PA (c/n 20354) emerged from Everett and was immediately stored at Wichita, Kansas, in July 1971. It was delivered to Pan Am on December 12, 1973, and served the airline until it entered storage again in the early 1990s. Mellon Financial Services Corporation acquired the aircraft and leased it to a number of airlines. Its last operator was Tower Air, which bought the aircraft and registered it as N609FF in August 1993. (David Stephens Collection)

Right: The Flying Tiger Line began 747 operations in 1974 and further expanded when it took over the aircraft operated by the Seaboard World cargo airline. Illustrated is one of the airline's 747-100s taken after the large 'T' logo was reinstated on the tail in 1987. The company has since been taken over by Federal Express. (Chris Penney)

Right: Belgian national carrier Sabena's first 747-129, OO-SGA (c/n 20401), is another example to undergo the upper deck modification to a ten window arrangement. This aircraft joined the airline on November 19, 1970, and was converted to SCD configuration in 1974. It was sold to the Tokyo Leasing Company in January 1986 and eventually broken up in October 1994. (Chris Penney)

Above: Tower Air 747-121 N604FF (c/n 19659) comes in to land at Los Angeles International Airport in October 1994. The aircraft was originally delivered to Pan Am as N755PA on May 31, 1970, and was bought by Tower Air in September 1988. After being leased to Garuda Indonesian Airways and Saudia, it was withdrawn from use at New York JFK International Airport in July 1998. (Airliner World – Dave Allport)

Left: Aer Lingus 747-148 EI-ASI, also sporting Air Jamaica titles on approach to London Heathrow. This aircraft joined the Irish carrier on December 15, 1970, and was sold to Global Aircraft Leasing in July 1991. Aer Lingus leased it back and continued operations until November 1994. It was subsequently purchased by Kabo Air of Nigeria in February 1997 and re-registered as 5N-ZZZ. (Chris Penney)

Left: During the 1991 Gulf War, a considerable number of 747s were utilised in support of Coalition troop movements to and from the Middle East. One aircraft involved was 747-122 N4714U (c/n 19876) of United Air Lines, seen here in Kuwait awaiting its next flight. The aircraft was finally retired in 1998 and used as a spares source. (Airliner World – Duncan Cubitt)

Right: Lion Air leased 747-121 LX-GCV from Cargolux in April 1988 and used the aircraft until March 1990 when it went to Air France on another leasing contract. It was first delivered as N770PA to Pan Am on May 31, 1970, bearing the name 'Clipper Great Republic'. In keeping with many Pan Am aircraft, the name changed on more than one occasion, first to 'Clipper Bald Eagle' in 1976 and then to 'Clipper Queen of the Pacific' in 1982. (Nigel Prevett)

Right: N602FF (c/n 19734) was first delivered to Continental Air Lines on July 13, 1970, as N26862, but was put into store by the airline in January 1974. It was then bought back by Boeing before being leased to a succession of operators. Among these was Air Europe which utilised the aircraft between May 1989 and February 1990. (Nigel Prevett)

Right: Okada Air was formed in 1983 and operated regional and charter flights from Nigeria. The airline bought its sole 747-146 (JA8102) from Japan Air Lines, 5N-EDO (c/n 19726), on May 28, 1992, and operated it until 1998 when, after a period of storage, it was leased by Summit Aviation in January 1998. It is seen here at London Stansted on December 19, 1992. (Nigel Prevett)

Right: A good example of the longevity of the original 747-100 design is 747-146F N702CK (c/n 20332), converted for Japan Air Lines in September 1977 having been delivered as a standard 747-146 (JA8107) on October 28, 1970. It was subsequently purchased by American International Airways on August 21, 1992 – that company's name changed to Kitty Hawk International in February 1999. (Nigel Prevett)

747SR

The SR (Short Range) version of the 747-100 evolved to fulfil the ever-growing need for increased capacity on the domestic Japanese routes. This business boomed during the 1960s and although it was intended to satisfy it with stretched 727s, Boeing quickly saw that a high capacity version of the 747 was far more practical. Japan Air Lines placed a $44 million order for four SRs on October 30, 1972.

The new aircraft was designed for short-range, high-cycle operations and, as a result, the airframe was extensively strengthened, notably around the wings and flying control surfaces, as well as the undercarriage. Because of the short, 200-500 mile (321-804km) flights, the aircraft would soon notch up a high number of landing and take-off cycles. The standard -100 was designed for 24,600 cycles during a planned 20-year life – the -100SR would achieve 52,000 cycles on high-density flights within Japan and so was modified to absorb the increased stresses on the airframe.

Originally the aircraft were configured to carry 482 passengers in a single-class layout, however by reducing the seat pitch they later carried up to 528 passengers. The first aircraft, designated as a 747SR-46 (c/n 20781, registration JA8117), was delivered to Japan Air Lines on September 26, 1973, the same day as the type received its FAA supplemental flight certificate. JAL introduced the aircraft on its Tokyo-Okinawa route on October 7, 1973. Powerplants comprised four Pratt & Whitney JT9D-7s rated at 43,500lb (193.48kN) of thrust. It is worth noting that the -100SR aircraft were the only new-build -100s to feature ten windows on the upper deck, as became standard on the -200, though many -100s eventually received this modification .

JAL's rival, All Nippon Airlines, consequently ordered the upgraded 747-100B which featured more powerful General Electric CF6-45A engines, the first of which flew on November 3, 1978. Eventually, ANA operated 17 747SR-81s, while JAL also ordered three more aircraft, powered by the Pratt & Whitney JT9D, that were designated as 747-146B(SR)s.

The SR concept was revived with the 747-300, again for the Japanese market, and most recently as the 747-400D (Domestic), though only in limited numbers. The -400D is not fitted with winglets because these only give significant fuel saving benefits during the long-distance cruise, something not attained on the short domestic flights. However, kit supplied winglets can be fitted to the aircraft to convert them to the standard -400 configuration for long-haul flights. This allows the airframes to be 'rotated', thus ensuring a spread of cycles across the fleet. As the number of cycles increased, many of the original aircraft were sold on to other operators, including a number of cargo airlines. One interesting operator is NASA, which acquired former Japan Air Lines 747SR-46 (c/n 20781, original registration JA8117) in October 1988 as N911NA for use as a Space Shuttle carrier aircraft. This aircraft supplemented an earlier NASA Boeing 747-123, N905NA (c/n 20107, original registration N9668), that it purchased from American Airlines in 1974.

747SR OPERATORS

- All Nippon Airways
- American International Airways
- Atlas Air
- Evergreen International Airlines
- Japan Air Lines
- NASA
- Nippon Cargo Airlines
- Qatar Airways
- Saudi Arabian Airlines
- United Parcel Service

747SR SPECIFICATIONS (with JT9D-7 engines)

Wingspan	195ft 8in (59.6m)
Length	231ft 4in (70.5m)
Height	63ft 5in (19.47m)
Wing area	5,500sq ft (511m²)
Weight empty (min)	348,816lb (158,223kg)
Weight maximum	520,000lb (235,870kg) – 735,000lb (333,400kg)
Fuel capacity	47,210 – 53,160 US gal (178,690 – 201,210 litres)
Cruising speed	550mph (884km/h)
Ceiling	45,000ft (13,700m)
Range	2,300 miles (3,700km)
Passenger capacity	Max 528

Below: All Nippon Airways 747-481D JA8955 (c/n 25639) comes in to land at Osaka Kansai in 1998. By then, the aircraft had been fitted with the kit-form winglets for use on non-domestic services. It was originally delivered to the airline as a -481D on May 12, 1992, and converted to a standard -481 in December 1996. (Robbie Shaw)

Right: Apart from those serving the Japanese market, very few airlines have flown versions of the SR. In fact all of these have procured the aircraft second-hand, such as Qatar Airways, which purchased this 747SR-81, A7-ABL (c/n 21605), seen here at Gatwick. The aircraft was delivered to All Nippon Airways on December 20, 1978, and remained with the airline until January 1995. This included a leased period from Aircraft Leasing, which bought it in March 1994. It was then bought by Boeing Equipment Holding and stored at Marana, Arizona, before passing to the Middle East airline on June 12, 1995. The operator leased it to Saudi Arabian Airlines from August 1997 until February 1999 and then sold it to AAR Aircraft & Engine Group Inc in April 1999. It has remained stored at Roswell, New Mexico, ever since. (Robbie Shaw)

Right: The 477th 747 built was 747SR-81 JA8147 (c/n 22293) for All Nippon Airways which received the aircraft on November 25, 1980. It has remained with the airline and is still in use today – it is seen here at Osaka-Itami on November 26, 1999. (Nigel Prevett)

Right: The -300 series 747 with its stretched upper deck was an obvious choice for the SR treatment. Japan Air Lines took delivery of 13 -346s, four of which were delivered as -346SRs including JA8187 (c/n 24019), seen here at Osaka-Itami wearing a special 'Super Resorts Express Okinawa' livery in early 1998. (Robbie Shaw)

Above: This aircraft, N911NA (c/n 20781), is used as a Space Shuttle carrier by NASA – this is easily the most unusual use for the SR variant, or indeed for any 747. It was delivered to Japan Air Lines as JA8117 on September 26, 1973, and was bought back by Boeing Equipment Holding in April 1988. NASA purchased the aircraft on October 27, 1988, and converted it to this configuration. Obvious modifications are the attachment points on the fuselage roof, and numerous refuelling stops are required when ferrying the Space Shuttle from Edwards AFB, California, to the Kennedy Space Center in Florida. The aircraft is often on static display at the annual Edwards AFB Open House – where it was photographed in October 1997. (Airliner World – Dave Allport)

Below: JA8148, an All Nippon Airways 747SR-81, taxies to the terminal at Haneda, Japan, on November 19, 1996. The large passenger capacity of the SRs was of significant importance for domestic Japanese routes. Without this aircraft, high-density Boeing 727s would have been used, necessitating many more flights to move the same number of people. (Nigel Prevett)

Right: The -400 series continued the SR theme but this time under the name 'Domestic'. Once again only Japanese operators have taken the aircraft – eight going to Japan Air Lines and eleven to All Nippon Airways. 747-446D JA8084 (c/n25214) is seen at Osaka Itami in early 1998 preparing for departure on another internal flight. (Robbie Shaw)

Right: ANA 747SR-81 JA8137 (c/n 21923) is pushed back at Kagoshima on November 25, 1996. The aircraft was delivered to All Nippon Airways on September 5, 1979, and then sold to N I Aircraft Leasing on March 15, 1995. It was immediately leased back by the airline and remained in use until it was purchased by Atlas Air in February 1999 and re-registered as N8078Q. It was flown to McConnell AFB in Kansas and broken up for spares in June 1999. (Nigel Prevett)

Right: One of the last -481Ds to be delivered to All Nippon Airways was JA8963 (c/n 25647), which was taken charge of by the airline on August 31, 1993. However, less than a month later, on September 10, it was sold to Fuyo Sogo Lease & Mitsui Lease Jigyo, and immediately leased back to the airline. The aircraft is illustrated wearing a rather attractive aquatic-style colour scheme. (Airliner World collection)

⑤ 747SP

The 747SP (Special Performance) initially came about to meet competition from Lockheed Martin with its new TriStar and McDonnell Douglas with its DC-10. Both of these aircraft were aimed at medium-range flights with a passenger capacity of 250-300, falling between the Boeing 707 and the larger 747. After looking at the possibility of designing a completely new aircraft, Boeing decided that a more cost-effective option would be to produce a shortened version of the 747, an idea that reversed the more usual trend to make aircraft even bigger. The result was the 747SP, some 48ft 4in (14.7m) shorter than the standard 747 (though still longer than the largest 707) but with increased tail span and a taller tail-fin. Actually there were far more structural changes and redesign needed than one might think but the resultant aircraft had a phenomenal performance. Not only did it meet the requirements to compete with the TriStar and DC-10, but it also had an exceptional range. This was because the fuel capacity was the same as the standard 747 but the weight of the SP was significantly less – 45,000lb (20,412kg) lighter than a 747-200B – and it generated less drag. One of the most significant weight saving measures was the replacement of the triple-slotted flaps with more conventional single flap units – which had practically no adverse effect on the aircraft's low-speed handling and landing performance.

Joe Sutter and his team worked hard to produce the aircraft, with Boeing formally announcing the programme in September 1973. Originally called the SB (short body) but replaced by SP after Pan Am dubbed the aircraft 'Sutter's Balloon', the first example flew on July 4, 1975. Pan Am wanted the aircraft for use on long-haul routes that needed less capacity than the standard 747 and so the aircraft soon became focused on this market rather than the medium-haul one.

Passenger capacity was typically around 280 in a mixed class layout. This capacity and performance level were relatively cheap for the airlines, since spares, support, main-

747SP SPECIFICATIONS	
Wingspan	195ft 8in (59.6m)
Length	184ft 9in (56.3m)
Height	65ft 5in (19.9m)
Wing area	5,500sq ft (511m²)
Weight empty (min)	383,400lb (173,900kg)
Weight maximum	690,000lb (313,000kg)
Fuel capacity	47,210 – 53,160 US gal
	(178,690 – 201,210 litres)
Cruising speed	619mph (996km/h)
Ceiling	45,000ft (13,700m)
Range	10,222 miles (16,400km)
Passenger capacity	305
Powerplants	choice of:
	4 x Pratt & Whitney JT9D-7A
	4 x Rolls-Royce RB211-524D4

tenance and crew training were all common to the 747-100/200s already in service. But it was the aircraft's long-range performance that was its real selling point along with its ability to cruise at higher altitudes and higher speeds than competing aircraft.

A demonstration flight for Japan Air Lines on November 12, 1975, went non-stop from New York to Tokyo, a distance of 6,927 miles (11,147km), in 13 hours 33 minutes, cruising at up to 46,000ft (14,020m) and Mach 0.86. Upon arrival in Tokyo, it still had 30,000lb (13,608kg) of fuel remaining. This opened up hitherto unheard of point-to-point services around the globe.

As with the original 747, Pan American Airways was the launch customer for the SP but despite sales predictions for as many as 214 examples between 1976-85, only 44 ever materialised – almost half of these were originally delivered to Pan Am. Interestingly, Boeing built a 45th SP some five years after normal production had ceased, to meet a special order from the United Arab

Right: Mandarin Airlines 747SP-09 B-1862 (c/n 21300) banks over the Hong Kong skyline on approach to Kai Tak International Airport on November 20, 1997. This aircraft was delivered to China Airlines on April 6, 1977, and leased to Mandarin Airlines between December 1992 and February 1999. It is now with Air Gulf Falcon as 5Y-GFC. (Nigel Prevett)

Right: France-based Corsair began life in 1981 as Corse Air International, flying four SE-210 Caravelles. It acquired its first 747-100 in 1990, and the following year adopted the Corsair name. The airline has flown almost every type of 747, except the SR and -400; illustrated is 747SP-44 F-GTOM (c/n 21253) undergoing maintenance at Paris Charles de Gaulle in 2000. The airline acquired the aircraft in October 1994 from Royal Air Maroc but it was originally delivered to South African Airways as ZS-SPE on November 22, 1976. (Airliner World – Ken Delve)

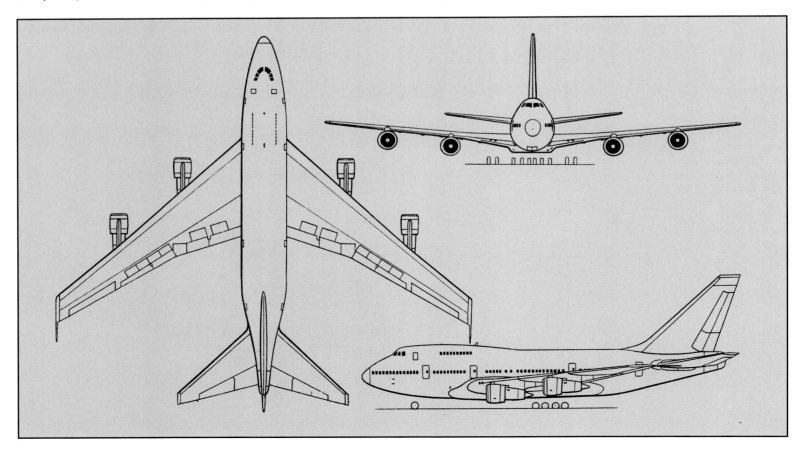

Emirates. Ironically, it was partly the increasing capabilities of the standard 747-200 that helped to seal the fate of the SP – as the bigger aircraft was developed so that its range and payloads increased, allowing it to achieve the ranges of the specialised 747SP.

Arguably one of the most interesting SPs still flying is former United Airlines 747SP-21 N145UA (c/n 21441 originally N536PA of Pan Am). This has been converted into a flying Stratospheric Observatory For Infrared Astronomy (SOFIA), a joint NASA/German space agency project, by the Universities Space Research Association (USRA) and Raytheon E-Systems. It carries an 8ft 2in (2.46m) diameter infrared telescope situated in the rear port side of the fuselage.

Today only around 25 SPs remain in service, including some configured as VIP aircraft for governments, but in total almost 50 different operators have utilised the type during its career.

747SP OPERATORS

Abu Dhabi Government	Braniff Airways	Kazakhstan Government	Saudi Arabian Airlines nee
Aerolineas Argentinas	Brunei Government	Korean Air	Saudia
Air Atlanta Icelandic	Cameroon Airlines	Korean Air Lines	Saudi Arabian Government
Air China	China Airlines	Luxair	South African Airways
Air Gulf Falcon	Civil Aviation Administration of	Mandarin Airlines	Syrianair
Air Malawi	China	Namib Air	Tajik Air
Air Mauritius	Corsair	NASA	Trans World Airlines
Air Namibia	Comores Airlines	Oman Government	Union de Transports Aeriens
Alliance Air	Dubai Government	Pan American World Airways	United Air Lines
American Airlines	Flitestar	Qantas	Yemen Government
Australia Asia Airlines	Iran Air	Qatar Airways	
Avia Airlines	Iraqi Airways	Qatar Government	
Bahrain Government	Kazakhstan Airlines	Royal Air Maroc	

747SP STATUS

C/n	Operator	Registration	Current Status	C/n	Operator	Registration	Current Status
20998	Iran Air	EP-IAA	Active	21786	Yemen Government	7O-YMN	Active
20999	Iran Air	EP-IAB	Active				
21022	United	N140UA	Dismantled	21932	Air China	N135SW	Stored Marana, AZ
21023	United	N141UA	Dismantled	21933	UT Finance Corp	N136SW	Stored Victorville
21024	United	N142UA	Dismantled				
21025	United	N143UA	Dismantled	21934	UT Finance Corp	N139SW	Plattsburg, NY
21026	United	N144UA	Dismantled				
21093	Iran Air	EP-IAC	Active	21961	United Arab Emirates	A6-SMR	Active
21132	South African	ZS-SPA	Active				
21133	Panair	N747KS (ZS-SPB)	Stored Marana, AZ	21962	VIP	P4-AFE	Stored Luxembourg
				21963	United Arab Emirates	A6-SMM	Active
21134	South African	ZS-SPC	Active				
21174	Syrianair	YK-AHA	Active	21992	Oman Government	A4O-SP	Active
21175	Syrianair	YK-AHB	Active				
21253	Corsair	F-GTOM	Active	22298	Iraqi Airways	5Y-GFD	Active
21254	South African	ZS-SPE	Active	²2302	Comores Airlines	D6-OZX	Active
21263	Air Mauritius	ZS-SPF	Scrapped				
21300	Air Gulf Falcon	5Y-GFC	Active	22483	Boeing	N709BA	Stored Marana, AZ
				22484	Boeing	N708BA	Stored Marana, AZ
21441	NASA	N145UA	SOFIA conversion, Waco, TX	22495	Qantas	VH-EAA	Stored
				22503	Saudia	HZ-AIF	Active
21547	United	N146UA	Stored Marana, AZ	22547	Mandarin Airlines	N4508H	Stored Marana, AZ
21548	FAA	N147UA	Testing ACV				
21648	Qatar Government	VP-BAT	Active	22672	Qantas	VH-EAB	Stored
				22750	Saudia Royal Flight	HZ-AIJ	Active
21649	Bahrain Amiri Flight	A9C-HHH	Active				
				22805	Mandarin Airlines	N4522V	Stored Las Vegas
21652	Saudi Arabian Government	HZ-HM1B	Active				
				22858	Iraqi	YI-ALM	Stored Tozeur
21758	Iran Air	EP-IAD	Active	23610	United Arab Emirates	A6-ZSN	Active
21785	Oman Government	A4O-SO	Active				

Details correct to January 2002.

Below: The first 747SP, 747SP-21 N747SP (c/n 21022), was originally used by Boeing for flight test and development before it joined Pan Am as N530PA on April 26, 1976. From February 1986 the aircraft joined United Air Lines and was re-registered N140UA in July that year. Sadly it was eventually broken up at Ardmore, Oklahoma, in March 1996. (Boeing)

Left: The SOFIA flying telescope project is one of the more unusual uses for the SP airframe. The aircraft, c/n 21441, was originally delivered to Pan Am as N536PA on May 6, 1977. United Air Lines acquired it in February 1986 and after nine years of service, it was put into storage in late 1995. In 1997 it was procured for the SOFIA project and registered to the Universities Space Research Association (USRA) on April 30, 1997. The aircraft is being modified and fitted with an infrared telescope in the specially-modified rear port fuselage. It will fly at up to 45,000ft (13,716m), way above most of the Earth's atmospheric pollution, thus providing scientists with an excellent research platform. (USRA/NASA)

Right: 747SP-44 ZS-SPF (c/n 21263) joined South African Airways on January 31, 1977, and during its career it was leased to a number of operators. Among these was Air Namibia, which leased the aircraft between April 1990 and April 1998. After returning to its original owner it was damaged beyond repair at Maputo, Mozambique, on October 5, 1998, and has since been scrapped. (Airliner World collection)

Right: Braniff Airways, famous for its colourful paint schemes, was one of the early customers for the SP. Here 747SP-27 N606BN (c/n 21992) taxies for departure at London Gatwick on July 22, 1981. This aircraft joined Pan Am on September 23, 1983, and was re-registered N529PA in January 1984. A spell with United Air Lines between February 1986 and August 1992 was followed by a VIP conversion for use by the Omani Royal Flight as A40-SP. (Nigel Prevett)

Below: A40-SP as it is today with the Omani Royal Flight. (Robbie Shaw)

Above: One of the few SPs to remain with its original customer, 747SP-38 VH-EAA (c/n 22495), joined Qantas on January 19, 1981, and remained in use with the Australian carrier until November 2001. The SP's superior long-range performance made it a popular choice to undertake some of the longest routes flown by the airline. VH-EAA is seen here at Sydney on October 16, 1988. (Nigel Prevett)

Above left: Syrian Arab Airlines 747SP-94 YK-AHB (c/n 21175) at Sharjah in late 1999. The aircraft was delivered to the Middle Eastern operator on July 16, 1976, and is still in use on international services. (Airliner World – Ken Delve)

Centre left: 747SP-21 N533PA (c/n 21025) was the fourth for Pan Am and was delivered on March 5, 1976. As is common among Pan Am's aircraft, it wore a number of names in the 'Clipper' series and it is seen here at London Heathrow as 'Clipper Young America', this name was current between 1980 and 1983. The aircraft was sold to United Air Lines in February 1986 to become N143UA, but was eventually broken up for spares at Ardmore, Oklahoma, in August 1995. (Chris Penney)

Left: Iran Air 747SP-86 EP-IAA (c/n 20998) arriving at London Heathrow in late 1998. The airline has used the aircraft since delivery on March 12, 1976, for international services. (Robbie Shaw)

Above: Another good example of a short-term lease contract, this 747SP-44 ZS-SPC (c/n 21134) was delivered to South African Airways on June 16, 1976, and has remained in the airline's ownership to this day. However, it has been leased to a number of operators, including Avia Airlines, which leased it between May and August 1995. (Robbie Shaw)

Above right: Boeing 747SP-44 c/n 21134 once again, this time as 3B-NAG when leased to Air Mauritius – it operated the aircraft from October 1984 until November 1994. (Nigel Prevett)

Right: The final SP built was 747SP-Z5 A6-ZSN (c/n 23610) which first flew on March 31, 1987 and was delivered to the United Arab Emirates Government on December 9, 1989. It is seen here about to touch down in Dubai in November 1999. (Airliner World – Ken Delve)

Right: Boeing 747SP-44 ZS-SPA (c/n 21132) joined South African Airways on March 19, 1976, and is one of many remaining with an African operator. The aircraft spent some time with Air Mauritius, and in February 1995 it was leased by Alliance Air, which applied this attractive livery. (Nigel Prevett)

Left: China was another customer for the SP, depicted here is Civil Aviation Administration of China (CAAC) 747SP-J6 B-2442 (c/n 21932) at London Gatwick on August 2, 1981. The aircraft was transferred to Air China on July 1, 1988, but eventually returned to the USA and is currently stored at Marana, Arizona. (Nigel Prevett)

Left: Boeing 747SP-B5 HL7456 (c/n 22483) of Korean Air at Moscow on August 29, 1993. This aircraft entered service in early 1981 but was returned to the Boeing Aircraft Holding Company as N709BA in November 1998 and is one of many SPs stored at Marana, Arizona. (Nigel Prevett)

Left: This 747SP-44 was originally delivered to South African Airways as ZS-SPB (c/n 21133) on April 22, 1976. In April 1985 it was leased to Air Malawi as 7Q-YKL for just one month, consequently images of it in Air Malawi colours are rare. The aircraft resorted to its original owner and registration, and was leased to several operators, including Luxair (as LX-LGX) between November 1987 and September 1993. It was eventually bought by Panair Inc in July 1999 and stored at Marana, Arizona. (Nigel Prevett)

Left: N141UA (c/n 21023) was the second SP to be completed and first flew on August 14, 1975, as N247SP – one of the Boeing flight test aircraft. It then joined Pan Am as N531PA until being sold to United Air Lines in February 1986. The aircraft ended its days being broken up at Ardmore, Oklahoma, but the rear fuselage was used as a design engineering mock-up for the Stratospheric Observatory For Infrared Astronomy (SOFIA) programme under a team led by NASA. (Robbie Shaw)

Above: South African Airways 747SP-44 ZS-SPE (c/n 21254) at Johannesburg in September 2000 displaying the latest livery to be carried by the airline's aircraft. Only three SPs currently remain in use by the airline. (Airliner World - Tony Dixon)

Right: This exotically painted 747SP-21, VR-BAT (c/n 21648), is currently registered to the Worldwide Aircraft Holding Company with a Bermuda registration and is leased to the Qatar Government. It started its service life with Pan Am in April 1979 as N539PA and, as with the other Pan Am SPs, joined United Air Lines in February 1986, and its current owner in October 1995. (Nigel Prevett)

Right: Boeing 747SP-31 N601AA (c/n 21962) commences its take-off run at London Heathrow. American Airlines purchased the aircraft from TWA in July 1986 and later sold it and re-leased it. The airline continued to operate the aircraft until July 1992. It has seen a number of owners and operators since then and is currently stored in Luxembourg. (David Stephens collection)

⑥ CONSTRUCTION

In order to build the world's largest airliner, Boeing had to construct the world's largest building. A site adjacent to Paine Field in Everett, Washington, was settled upon and construction of a huge assembly hall began in mid-1966. When completed, it was the world's largest building by volume, with an internal space of 472 million cu ft (13.3 million m³), a record it still holds today following two extensions to permit assembly of the newer 767 and 777 airliners.

Putting together an aircraft the size of the 747 is no quick and easy job. The aircraft contains in excess of six million parts and more than 140 miles of wiring. Each part and each piece of wire must arrive at the correct point along the construction line at precisely the right time. Sixty-five per cent of the aircraft arrives at Everett as sub-assemblies, coming from sub-contractors across the US and overseas.. All these, together with air conditioning ducts, piping, instruments, communications equipment, engines, undercarriage and a host of other items, are then put together in a precise order. To make it easier to put together such a massive jigsaw puzzle, an incredible 270,000 different manufacturing tools are required, ranging from small hand-held items to huge wing jigs and fuselage assembly bays. The result emerges from the assembly building and passes on to the paint shop and flight test.

Below: Building a 747 is engineering on a colossal scale. Here the front and centre fuselage sections are mated at Everett as other 747s pass down the assembly line. (Boeing)

Right: The 747th Boeing 747, 747-430M combi D-ABTA (c/n 24285) for Lufthansa, comes together at Everett in 1989. Here the horizontal stabiliser, manufactured by LTV Aircraft Products Group in Dallas, Texas, is being attached: this unit contains fuel tanks with a capacity of 22,110lb (10,029kg). The supplier is one of hundreds which provide parts, components or larger sub-assemblies for the 747 and other Boeing products. (Boeing)

Right: The intricate work which goes into the manufacture of any airliner is seldom seen by the public. Here just a fraction of the miles of wiring in a 747 are plumbed into the lower cargo hold of a fuselage sub-assembly at Everett in October 2000. (Airliner World – Mark Nicholls)

Left: Birthplace of every Boeing 747 – the massive assembly building at Everett, Washington, north of Seattle. The original part of the building is the three bays to the left. The next bay was added for the 767 line and the two on the right for the 777 line. (Boeing)

Right: A 747-400F undergoes the final fuselage join at Everett in October 2000. It is a remarkable experience to see literally thousands of parts come together and emerge as an aircraft. But as is evident from the signs around the aircraft, great care is taken to maintain a safe working environment in the massive factory. (Airliner World – Mark Nicholls)

747-200

Even before the first 747 was built, Boeing was studying an increased range variant of the 747, known as the 747B. This eventually became known as the 747-200 – and while it retained the same dimensions as the -100, it had an increased fuel capacity. This increase required extensive strengthening of the aircraft's structure, from the wings and fuselage, right down to the undercarriage and even the tyres. As a result, the new aircraft had a higher maximum take-off weight of 775,000lb (351,540kg) and was initially powered by water injected P&W JT9D-3AWs, as used on the -100; though these were soon replaced by JT9D-7s. However, it was not long before both General Electric and Rolls-Royce offered engines of their own, and as all three manufacturers continued to develop more powerful products, so the maximum take-off weights continued to increase. Indeed, while testing the Rolls-Royce RB211-524-02, a 747-283B established a new weight record of 840,500lb (381,250kg) on November 1, 1976.

The only obvious visible difference between the -200 and the earlier -100 were the ten windows provided for the upper deck. This was because the number of seats there had been increased to 16, though some -100SRs for Japan also had the same window configuration and indeed many -100s also had their upper decks modified to include the ten-window arrangement. Gone were the days of using the upper deck as a lounge area, airlines saw the revenue potential of adding more seats here, usually for Business Class.

With the -200 appearing during 1971 it is not surprising that many airlines saw the potential it offered and converted many existing orders for -100s into -200s. The first -200 was the 88th 747 (c/n 20356) to roll off the Everett production line, on August 27, 1970. Following extensive testing it was delivered to Northwest Orient as N611US on March 26, 1971.

Competition between the three big engine manufacturers eventually saw the maximum take-off weight soar to well over 800,000lb (362,880kg) with a large amount of the extra weight made up of fuel. This meant that the later variants could fly around 1,000 miles (1,609km) further than the earliest P&W powered -200s with the same payload.

The American military also found uses for the 747 and the US Air Force took delivery of six -200 variants, four as E-4A/B airborne command posts and two as VC-25A Presidential transports. All of these remain in use with the USAF, the E-4Bs now based at Offutt AFB, Nebraska, and the two VC-25As at Andrews AFB, Maryland.

It was also during the -200 phase of 747 production, that other military versions were proposed. One was as an air-to-air refuelling tanker, while others saw its possible use as an air-launched cruise missile (ALCM) platform or an inter-continental ballistic missile (ICBM) launch platform. In the event none materialised, though it was thought by many that the tanker version would

747-200 SPECIFICATIONS

Wingspan	195ft 8in (59.6m)
Length	231ft 10in (70.65m)
Height	63ft 5in (19.47m)
Wing area	5,500sq ft (511m^2)
Weight empty (min)	374,700lb (170.000kg)
Weight maximum	833,000lb (377.800kg)
Fuel capacity	47,210 – 53,160 US gal (178,690 – 201,210 litres)
Cruising speed	604mph (972km/h)
Ceiling	40,000ft (12,000m)
Range	7,940 miles (12,775km)
Passenger capacity	Maximum of 550
Powerplants	choice of 4 x Pratt & Whitney JT9D-74R4G2 4 x General Electric CF6-50E2 4 x Rolls-Royce RB211-524D4-B

Opposite page, top: China Airlines 747-209F B-160 (c/n 24308) makes a typically spectacular approach to the old Hong Kong Kai Tak airport in December 1997. This aircraft was delivered to the airline on August 29, 1989, and now sports the smart new livery introduced in 1995. (Robbie Shaw)

Opposite page, bottom: Atlas Air commenced operations in 1992 and now operates a fleet of over 20 747-100s, -200s (as shown here) and -400s. It offers a worldwide service, as well as charter availability to other airlines and is one of many dedicated cargo airlines using the 747. (Airliner World – Ken Delve)

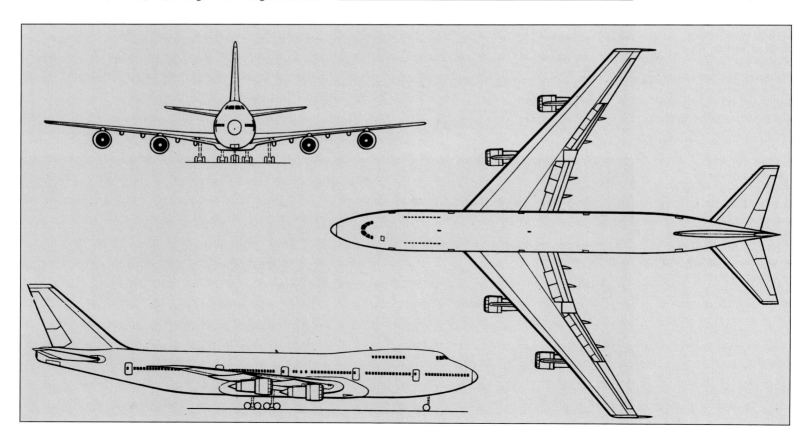

have had much merit due to the amount of fuel it could have carried.

Today many -200s continue to provide reliable service to many of the world's airlines, though their retirement has been speeded up following the September 11, 2001, terrorist attacks on the USA. Considering the 747 was aimed solely at the long-haul market it is quite staggering that so far the -200 has served with 123 operators. The final -200 was a -200F freighter, the 393rd -200 series to emerge from the Everett production line, which was delivered to Nippon Air Cargo in November 1991.

747-200 OPERATORS

Aerolineas Argentinas	Continental Airlines	Nationair
Air Afrique	Continental Micronesia	Nigeria Airways
Air Algerie	Corsair	Nippon Cargo Airlines
Air Atlanta Icelandic	Corse Air International	Northwest Airlines nee Northwest Orient Airlines
Air Canada	CP Air	
Air China	Dubai Air Wing	Olympic Airways
Air Club International	Egypt Air	Overseas National
Air France	El Al	Pakistan International Airlines
Air Gabon	Evergreen International Airlines	Pan American World Airways
Air Gulf Falcon	Federal Express	People Express Airlines
Air Hong Kong	Flying Tiger Line	Philippine Airlines
Air India	Fortunair Canada	Polar Air Cargo
Air Inter	Garuda Indonesian Airways	Qantas
Air Lanka	German Cargo	Qatar Airways
Air Madagascar	Gulf Air	Royal Air Maroc
Air New Zealand	Hydro Air	Royal Jordanian Airlines
Air Pacific	Iberia	Sabena
Airasia	(Imperial) Iranian Air Force	Saha Airlines
Airfreight Express	Iran Air	Saudi Arabian Airlines nee Saudia
Airtours International Airways	Iraqi Airways	Scanair
Alia Royal Jordanian Airlines	Jalways	Scandinavian Airlines System
Alitalia	Japan Air Charter	Singapore Airlines
All Nippon Airways	Japan Air Lines	South African Airways
America West Airlines	Japan Asia Airways	Southern Air Transport and successor Southern Air
American Airlines	Japan Universal System Transport	
American International Airways	Kabo Air	Swissair
AOM French Airlines	Kalitta Air	TAP Air Portugal
Atlas Air	Kitty Hawk International	Thai Airways International
Avianca	KLM Royal Dutch Airlines	Tower Air
Braniff Airways	Korean Air nee Korean Air Lines	Trans World Airlines
British Airtours	Kuwait Airways	Transamerica Airlines
British Airways	Libyan Arab Airlines (leased, order cancelled)	Transportes Aereos Portugueses
British Caledonian Airways	Lion Air	Tunis Air
Caledonian Airways	LTU Lufttransport-Unternehmen	Union de Transports Aeriens
Cameroon Airlines	Lufthansa	United Air Lines
Canadian Pacific Air Lines	Lufthansa Cargo	United Parcel Service
Cargo Air Lines	Malaysian Airline System	United States Air Force
Cargolux	Martinair Holland	Varig
Cathay Pacific Airways	Metro International Airways	Viasa
China Airlines	Middle East Airlines	Virgin Atlantic Airways
Civil Aviation Administration of China	Minerve	Wardair Canada
Condor	MK Airlines	World Airways

Right: Philippine Airlines took delivery of 747-2F6B N744PR (c/n 22382) on December 12, 1980. The airline has since replaced its -200s with -400s, this example was sold to the Polaris Aircraft Leasing Corporation in April 1996 and was last operated by Tower Air. (Chris Penney)

Centre right: This 747-2L5B, VR-HMF (c/n 22107), has an interesting history. It was originally ordered by Libyan Arab Airlines but not taken up. Instead, it went to Varig of Brazil on March 5, 1981, as PP-VNC but was sold to Orient Leasing in December 1982. It was then leased back to Varig for 12 years before entering a period of storage at Rio de Janeiro. Cathay Pacific then purchased it in February 1996 and it was converted to a freighter before being leased to Air Hong Kong in August 1996. It has since been re-registered again as B-HMF and is seen at Kai Tak prior to this. (Airliner World – Malcolm English)

Bottom right: This Air France Cargo 747-228F is another example of an airline buying, selling and then leasing the same aircraft. F-GCBM (c/n 24879) was delivered to Air France on November 30, 1990, and was then sold to US West Financial Services Ltd the same day. Air France leased it back and then sub-leased it, also on the same day, to UTA. It was returned to Air France on December 29, 1992. (Airliner World – Ken Delve)

Left: Martinair Holland (Martin's Luchtvervoer Maatschaappij) has operated 747-21AC PH-MCE (c/n 23652) from new since it was delivered on February 23, 1987. It was leased for two months to Virgin Atlantic Airways between February and April 1989 and is currently still in use by the Amsterdam Schiphol based airline. (Chris Penney)

Left: Yet another carrier that has long since passed into oblivion. Transamerica was originally called Trans International Airways (TIA) until 1976 and flew transatlantic charter flights between the US and Europe. Its 747s, including 747-271C N742TV (c/n 21965), were introduced in 1980, but the airline folded in 1986. This aircraft went on to serve Cargolux and Southern Air Transport before being sold to Atlas Air in December 1998 and re-registered as N539MC. (Chris Penney)

Top right: UK-based Virgin Atlantic Airways has considerably expanded its operations since the early 1980s. Among its first 747 acquisitions was this 747-287B G-VIRG (c/n 21189), purchased on June 14, 1984. The aircraft is seen here in June 1989 wearing the early Virgin livery. The only previous operator of this aircraft was Aerolineas Argentinas between 1976 and 1982. Virgin's -200 series were all withdrawn from use in the aftermath of the September 11, 2001, terrorist attacks on the USA. (Chris Penney)

Left: D-ABYT (c/n 22363), a 747-230B combi belonging to Lufthansa Cargo, comes in to land at Sharjah in May 1999. The aircraft was delivered to Lufthansa on November 19, 1980, and apart from a few changes to the operator's name, has remained with the German carrier ever since. (Airliner World – Dave Allport)

Bottom right: KLM 747-206B PH-BUP (c/n 22376) first flew on August 6, 1980, and was delivered to the Dutch airline on September 11 of the same year. It was returned to Boeing for the 'SUD' – Stretched Upper Deck – modification in December 1984, effectively bringing it up to the same specification as the 747-300. (Chris Penney)

Left: For a short period during the early 1990s, Air Club International leased two 747s. One was 747-212B C-GCIH (c/n 21162) illustrated here, and the other was 747-128 C-GCIS (c/n 20376). The former was originally delivered to Singapore Airlines on March 30, 1976, and was until recently operated by Tower Air as N620FF. (David Stephens Collection)

Left: Air New Zealand took delivery of this 747-219B, ZK-NZY (c/n 22725), on June 22, 1982, and it remained with the airline until it was replaced by new-build 747-419s. This aircraft has since joined UK-based Virgin Atlantic Airways as G-VPUF. (Chris Penney)

Right: Sporting the latest South African Airways (SAA) livery, 747-244B combi ZS-SAR was delivered to the airline on November 6, 1980, and apart from a two-year lease to Garuda Indonesian Airways between November 1992 and December 1994, has remained with SAA. It was converted to a freighter in September 1995 and is seen here at Johannesburg in 1999. (Airliner World – Tony Dixon)

Left: For a considerable period of its life, 747-2B4B combi N204AE (c/n 21099) was operated by African/Middle Eastern based airlines such as Middle East Airlines and, as shown here, Egyptair. It was originally delivered to Middle East Airlines on August 20, 1975 as OD-AGJ but became N204AE in 1985 – then after a series of leases to a number of airlines it was re-registered as N713CK with American International Airlines and converted to a freighter in October 1998. The current operator of this aircraft is Kitty Hawk International. (Chris Penney)

Centre right: This 747-259B combi was originally delivered to Avianca (Aerovias Nacionales de Colombia) on June 8, 1979, as HK-2300 (c/n 21730). It was subsequently purchased by Chemco International Leasing on May 30, 1983, and leased back to Avianca on the same date, re-registered as HK-2980X. It is seen here at Frankfurt, Germany, in mid-1985 and since then has passed through a number of owners, was converted to a freighter in 1998 and is currently registered to Aerousa Inc as N924FT which has leased the aircraft to Polar Air Cargo. (Chris Penney)

Right: 747-240B combi AP-BAK (c/n 21825) of Pakistan International Airlines was taken on charge by the airline on July 26, 1979. It is still in use by the airline and is seen here at Dubai in November 1999. (Airliner World – Alan Warnes)

Left: For a -200 series Jumbo, this example is one of a very few to have only had one owner. Air Madagascar took delivery of 747-2B2B combi 5R-MFT (c/n 21614) on January 26, 1979 – the aircraft is still in operation with the airline some 22 years later and is seen here at Paris Orly in 1987. (Chris Penney)

Left: Fiji-based Air Pacific leased 747-238B DQ-FJE (c/n 22614) from Qantas initially in 1993 when it was still registered VH-EBR, and again on August 3, 1996, when it acquired the new registration. The aircraft is used on international routes in the Pacific region and is seen here on approach to Los Angeles International Airport. (Robbie Shaw)

Opposite page, top: The other major Japanese carrier, All Nippon Airways, also has a substantial 747 fleet including 747-281B JA8175 (c/n 23502) seen here at Frankfurt in June 1999. This aircraft was delivered to the airline on July 2, 1986. (Airliner World – Ken Delve)

Left: Japan Air Lines is the largest single 747 operator, with over 80 examples on its books and deliveries of the -400 variant continuing. JA8937 (c/n 22477) is a 747-246F that was originally delivered to the airline as JA8151 on April 15, 1981. It was then sold to the United Technologies International Corporation as N740SJ on August 25, 1994, and bought by a series of financial corporations before being leased back by Japan Air Lines on January 11, 1999. The aircraft is seen departing from Anchorage, Alaska, in May 2000. (Robbie Shaw)

Left: CP Air can trace its roots back to the formation of Canadian Pacific Airlines in 1942. This aircraft, 747-217B C-FCRB (c/n 20802), was delivered to the airline on December 3, 1973, and continued to serve it until being sold to Pakistan International Airlines as AP-BCM on May 19, 1986. CP Air disappeared together with many other smaller airlines during the formation of Canadian Airlines International in 1988. (Chris Penney)

Right: Boeing 747-283B combi SE-DFZ (c/n 21575) was delivered to Scandinavian Airline Systems (SAS) on March 2, 1979. Between June 3, 1983 and June 3, 1984, it was leased to Nigerian Airways which leased it again for periods during 1986, 1987 and 1988. It is pictured here at London Heathrow in May 1984. The aircraft was then sold and saw service with operators in Asia and South America before being converted to a freighter and sold to Polar Air Cargo in February 1997. It is currently with the operator as N921FT. (Chris Penney)

Right: Cathay Pacific 747-267B B-HIB (c/n 22149) comes in over the Hong Kong rooftops on approach to Kai Tak Airport during 1997. The special colour scheme depicting the Hong Kong skyline and the titles 'The Spirit of Hong Kong 97' was applied to the aircraft prior to the handing back of the colony to China in 1997. (Robbie Shaw)

Right Union de Transports Aeriens (UTA) 747-2B3F F-GBOX (c/n 21835) awaits its next flight at Frankfurt, Germany, in May 1985. The airline operated the aircraft from its delivery date on August 6, 1979, until the airline merged with Air France in December 1992. (Chris Penney)

Left: People Express was a low-cost airline that resembled Freddie Laker's Laker Airlines offering cheap international flights between the USA and the UK. The airline operated into London Gatwick, where this aircraft, N602PE (c/n 21682), was photographed in the company of a Northwest Airlines' 747 during the early 1980s. (Nigel Prevett)

Left: The Boeing -200 series saw a considerable number of new aircraft emerge as freighters, while many passenger versions have also been modified with either the SCD fit or to complete freighter specification. Here 747-281F JA8191 (c/n 24576) is about to touch down at Anchorage, Alaska in mid-2000. (Robbie Shaw)

Lower left: Iran Air 747-2J9F EP-ICB (c/n 21507) landing at London Heathrow in the mid-1980s. The Middle Eastern airline has also flown the -100 and SP versions of the Jumbo while many, including this one, have served with the Iranian Air Force as well. This aircraft was delivered to the Imperial Iranian air Force on September 29, 1978, and was leased to Iran Air between September 1980 and February 1988. (Nigel Prevett)

Bottom left: Lufthansa 747-230B combi D-ABYT (c/n 22363) was handed over to the German airline on November 11, 1980, and has effectively remained with the carrier ever since. It was transferred to Lufthansa Leasing AG in October 1989 and converted to a SCD freighter in August 1990. German Cargo Air leased the aircraft from August 30, 1990, and it has remained with it – though under two different names, Lufthansa Cargo Airlines and Lufthansa Cargo – before being purchased by Lufthansa Cargo in September 1998. The aircraft is pictured in German Cargo colours at Frankfurt in May 1992. (Nigel Prevett)

Right: The combi version of the -200 proved very popular with the airlines, offering considerable flexibility with the capability to carry a greater mix of passengers and cargo. August 1989 sees Kuwait Airways 747-269B combi 9K-ADC (c/n 21543) landing at London Heathrow. It was delivered to the airline on February 28, 1979, and stayed with it until December 1987, when it began a series of lease periods to a number of airlines including Egyptair and Garuda Indonesian Airways. It was sold to American International Airways as N708CK on June 29, 1995, and converted to a freighter. The operator now trades under the title Kitty Hawk International and the aircraft is still in use. (Nigel Prevett)

Right and lower right: Continental 747-238B N610PE has had a particularly interesting history. It was originally delivered to Qantas as VH-EBF 'City of Adelaide' on August 1, 1983. It was sold to the Boeing Equipment Holding Corporation in November 1985, leased back to Qantas and then sold to Peoples Express Airlines in December 1986. This airline merged with Continental Air Lines in February 1987, and the first image was taken during this period of ownership at Gatwick on October 2, 1987. Pegasus Capital Corporation acquired the aircraft in December 1989 but it remained leased to Continental until it was stored at Marana, Arizona, from March 1985. It was returned to use in October 1996 and sub leased to Continental Micronesia before returning to Continental in March 1999 and once more entering storage at Marana. (Nigel Prevett)

Bottom right Metro International Airways leased this 747-212B on several occasions during the early 1980s from Tigerair Inc and the Flying Tiger Line. The aircraft is seen during typically inclement northern European weather at Brussels on August 21, 1981. It was originally delivered to Singapore Airlines as 9V-SQC on July 29, 1974, and after its period with Metro International, it passed on to Pan Am, Aeronautics Leasing Inc and Pacific Harbor Capital Inc which leased it to a number of operators. It was converted to SCD specification in July 1987 and then to full freighter specification in 1993 – eventually being retired in October 1998. (Nigel Prevett)

Left: Iraqi Airways 747-270C YI-AGN (c/n 21180) on final approach to London Heathrow on April 15, 1983. The airline received the aircraft on June 24, 1976, and continued to operate it until it was seized by Iran in February 1991 during the Gulf War. The aircraft has remained in Iran and its fate is unknown, though most likely it has been used as a spares source for Iran Air and Iranian Air Force 747s. (Nigel Prevett)

Lower left: Swissair 747-257B HB-IGB (c/n 20117), the 126th 747 off the production line, is a good example of how the dual production of -100 and -200 aircraft led to some non-standard features. The upper deck of this Swissair aircraft is configured with three windows as in the original -100 series, although the majority of the -200 series was completed with the ten-window arrangement. Zurich, Switzerland, is the setting for this shot, taken on August 29, 1981. The airline received the aircraft on March 25, 1971, and after eleven years of use, sold it to Skips A/S Tudor in December 1982. It then passed to a number of owners and leasing companies before eventually being retired in September 1994 and broken up at Ardmore, Oklahoma. (Nigel Prevett)

Left: One of the few 747s to remain with one owner is 747-2Q2B combi F-ODJG (c/n 21468). Air Gabon took delivery of the aircraft as N1248E on October 5, 1978 – it was originally to have been registered as TR-LXK but this was not taken up. The aircraft was named 'President Leon Mba' in December 1978 and was pressed into service on the route to Paris Charles de Gaulle, where it was seen in November 1982. (Nigel Prevett)

Below left: Boeing 747-283B combi N4501Q of Scandinavian Airlines System (SAS) receives final instructions from the dispatcher at London Heathrow on September 4, 1983. Delivered on February 17, 1981, the aircraft was also leased by the airline to Egyptair before being sold to GPA Group Ltd in February 1988. It was then leased out and also passed through a number of leasing companies before finally being converted to a freighter in November 1997 and bought by United Parcels Service in February 1998 as N523UP. (Nigel Prevett)

Right: G-GAFX (c/n 20827), a 747-245F, comes in to land at London Heathrow on May 21, 2000. The aircraft is now operated by Airfreight Express, on lease from the Boeing Equipment Holding Corporation; this arrangement commencing in May 1999. The aircraft started life when it was delivered to Seaboard World Airlines as N702SW on April 30, 1976. (Nigel Prevett)

Right: Italy's Alitalia is one of many large airlines that operates freighter versions of the 747 alongside passenger aircraft. Boeing 747-243F I-DEMR (c/n 22545) was delivered to the airline on December 18, 1981, and is the sole -200F type it operates. (Nigel Prevett)

Right: Las Vegas McCarran International Airport in November 1992 is the setting for this shot of stored 747-206B N531AW, after it was retired by America West Airlines. The aircraft first served with KLM Royal Dutch Airlines after delivery as PH-BUA on January 16, 1971. Two leasing/finance companies bought the aircraft in 1996 but it has since been broken up at Kingman, Arizona. (Nigel Prevett).

Right: Japan Asia Airways 747-246B JA8155 (c/n 22746) at Narita on November 27, 1996. The aircraft was delivered to Japan Air Lines on December 15, 1981, and then sold to Japan Asia Airways on February 28, 1992. (Nigel Prevett)

747-300

The final version of what is commonly called the original 'classic' 747 was the -300, which came about as a result of continued pressure from airlines for more range and more passenger capacity. Actually the -200B was offered with a stretched upper deck (SUD) providing room for up to 91 economy passengers or 38 in Business Class from June 20, 1980. Although the extended upper cabin added some 10,000lb (4,536kg) of weight to the aircraft, the lengthened hump actually improved the aerodynamics and increased the cruise speed from Mach 0.84 to 0.85.

Launch customer for the -200B(SUD) was Swissair, with an order for four aircraft. When the first of these, a -357M combi version (c/n 22704 HB-IGC), was delivered to the customer on March 19, 1983, the designation had been changed to the 747-300. Only 81 -300s were produced, although the SUD was also applied to a pair of 747-146B(SR/SUD) aircraft, c/ns 22066 and 22067, registrations JA8142 and 8134 respectively, for Japan Air Lines in 1985. The breakdown of -300 production was 56 -300s, four -300SRs and 21 -300Ms (combis).

Boeing reached a deal with KLM in 1983 to convert some of its -206 aircraft to SUD configuration. This involved complete replacement of the upper forward fuselage sec-

tion and the finished aircraft were essentially completed as -300s. A total of ten aircraft were modified, three -206Bs and seven -206M combis, the work being performed between 1984 and 1986. A further two -200s were converted for French carrier UTA and this work helped Boeing to keep the 747 line open until the arrival of the -400.

747-300 SPECIFICATIONS	
Wingspan	195ft 8in (59.6m)
Length	231ft 10in (70.65m)
Height	63ft 5in (19.47m)
Wing area	5,500sq ft (511m²)
Weight empty (min)	383,400lb (173,900kg)
Weight maximum	833,000lb (377,800kg)
Fuel capacity	47,210 – 53,160 US gal (178,690 – 201,210 litres)
Cruising speed	619mph (996km/h)
Ceiling	45,000ft (13,700m)
Range	6,502 miles (10,500km)
Passenger capacity	Maximum of 563
Powerplants choice of	4 x Pratt & Whitney JT9D-74R4G4
	4 x General Electric CF6-80C2B1
	4 x Rolls-Royce RB211-524D4

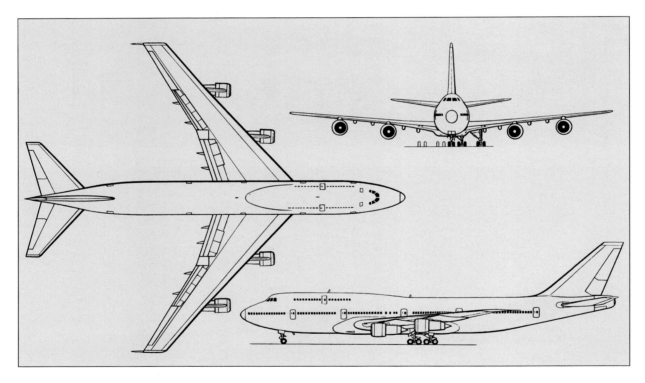

Opposite page, bottom: Korean Air Lines took delivery of three -300 aircraft, including 747-3B5M combi HL7470 (c/n 24194). This aircraft has remained with the airline since its arrival on August 30, 1988. The -300 combi version proved very popular with the airlines since the extra capacity of the stretched upper deck offset the use of part of the main passenger deck for cargo. (Chris Penney)

Below: South African Airways 747-344 ZS-SAU (c/n 22971) makes a classic curving approach to Hong Kong Kai Tak Airport in November 1994. (Robbie Shaw)

Below: Boeing 747-341 PP-VOA (c/n 24106) was delivered to the International Lease Finance Corporation on April 30, 1988, and then leased to Brazilian carrier Varig on the same day. The aircraft is seen in April 1989 still in the old colour scheme, which has recently been replaced by a more modern livery. Today the aircraft is registered to Air Atlantic Iceland as TF-ATH and leased to El Al. (Chris Penney)

747–300 OPERATORS

Aeromaritime International	Garuda Indonesian Airways	Saudi Arabian Airlines
Air Algerie	Iberia	Saudi Arabian Government
Air Atlanta Icelandic	Japan Air Lines	Saudia
Air France	Japan Asia Airways	Singapore Airlines
Air India	KLM Royal Dutch Airlines	South African Airways
Ansett Australia	Korean Air (Korean Air Lines)	Swissair
Atlas Air	Malaysian Airline System	TAAG Angola Airlines
Cathay Pacific Airways	Martinair Holland	Thai Airways International
Corsair	Pakistan International Airlines	Union de Transports Aeriens
Dragonair	Qantas	Varig
Egypt Air	Royal Air Maroc	Virgin Atlantic Airways
El Al	Sabena	

Left: Malaysian Airline System has just one -300 variant, 747-3H6M combi 9M-MHK (c/n 23600), seen here at Los Angeles International Airport in 1989. (Chris Penney)

Right: The largest single customer for the -300 was Singapore Airlines, which ordered 14 747-312s. N123KJ (c/n 23243) was delivered to the airline on April 30, 1985, and remained with it apart from a 15-day lease to Ansett Airlines of Australia in September 1996. This aircraft, seen here at Hong Kong Kai Tak airport in 1986, was taken out of use in January 1999. (Robbie Shaw)

Left: Nine of Japan Air Lines' 13 -300s are the standard 747-346s, the others are SR versions. JA8166 (c/n 23151) is seen coming in to land wearing the old colour scheme of the airline in 1987. The airline took delivery of the aircraft on February 4, 1985, and it remains in its service. (Chris Penney)

Right: KLM 747-306M combi PH-BUV (c/n 23137) taxies to its parking slot at Los Angeles International Airport on March 13, 1995, after arriving from Amsterdam Schiphol. KLM ordered three -306 aircraft but also returned ten of its GE CF6-50E2 powered -206B combi aircraft to Boeing to receive the stretched upper deck, effectively making them -306s as well. This was the 600th 747 produced and has remained with the Dutch national carrier throughout its carrier. (Nigel Prevett)

Left: Egyptair purchased two -300s, one of which, 747-366M combi SU-GAL (c/n 24161), is seen here at Cairo International. The airline uses these aircraft for long-haul services alongside 767, 777 and Airbus 340 aircraft. (Egyptair)

Right: Swissair was the launch customer for the -300 in 1980 when it placed an order for four aircraft, later increased to five. This example, 747-357M combi HB-IGC (c/n 22704), had already been ordered as a -200 but was fitted with the stretched upper deck and finished as a -357 – it was delivered to the airline on March 19, 1983. Swissair retired its 747s in January 2000 and disposed of them to a number of airlines, including TAAG Angola Airlines. This example has been stored at Marana, Arizona, as N270BC, since June 1999. (Chris Penney)

Left: Former Swissair 747-357M combi HB-IGG (c/n 23751) is now with TAAG Angola Airlines as D2-TEB – it is seen here at Johannesburg in September 2000. (Airliner World – Tony Dixon)

Right: Ansett Australia leased this aircraft, VH-INJ (c/n 23029), from Singapore Airlines between August 29, 1994 and August 11, 1998. The aircraft is seen here winging its way over the Hong Kong rooftops on approach to Kai Tak airport in October 1995. The aircraft was returned to Singapore Airlines as 9V-SKD but the airline has now retired its remaining -300s. (Robbie Shaw)

Lower left: Boeing 747-368 HZ-AIL (c/n 23263) of Saudi Arabian Airlines on finals at Los Angeles International Airport in December 2000. The aircraft which joined the airline, then called Saudia, on August 2, 1985, is still in use on long-haul flights and is one of ten operated by the airline, all powered by Rolls-Royce RB211 engines. (Robbie Shaw)

Right: The location is Brussels and the date, July 23, 1987, as a Sabena 747-329M combi is pushed back prior to departure. The aircraft, OO-SGC (c/n 23439), was one of two -300s delivered to the Belgian carrier, but it has now been sold to Aircraft 23439 LLC and registered N3439F. On December 1, 2000, it was ferried from Amsterdam to Tel Aviv for freighter conversion. (Nigel Prevett)

Bottom left: Apart from the military versions used by the US Air Force, this 747-3G1 of the Saudi Arabian Government is one of the more unusual 747s. Delivered to the operator as HZ-HM1A (c/n 23070) on December 22, 1983, it is clearly well equipped; note the satcom antenna housing on the roof behind the upper deck hump. Particularly rare, the aircraft is seen here at London Heathrow in May 1987. (Chris Penney)

Right: Qantas 747-338 VH-EBX (c/n 23688) is one of six RB211-powered aircraft used by the airline. It was delivered on November 12, 1986, and will eventually be replaced by the new 747-400ER – Qantas having ordered six in late 2000. (Chris Penney)

FREIGHTERS

Despite the fact that the 747 was originally designed primarily as a cargo aircraft, none of the -100 series was delivered as such, though some were dual passenger-cargo combi versions. This was because the airlines saw more immediate profit and expansion advantage from utilising the copious passenger-carrying capabilities of the aircraft. Another factor was the 1973/74 oil crisis which saw a downturn in passenger numbers and a number of aircraft put up for disposal. Many -100s were snapped up on the second-hand market and converted to -100SF (Special Freighter) specification by the Boeing-Wichita Modification Responsibility Center in Kansas. This involved the fitting of a side cargo door behind the port wing, though the limiting factor was the power of the engines which meant that most early modifications did not include the hinged nose door due to the extra weight penalty.

However, the arrival of the -200 series with its more powerful engines, increased payload and maximum take-off weights, offered more capabilities to the cargo carriers. Some 73 -200Fs were built from new and the type continued in production until 1991 when it was replaced by the -400F. During this period, and indeed since, a significant number of passenger -200s were modified to -200Fs. The first -200F was D-ABYE (c/n 20373), a 747-230F for

Lufthansa, which was rolled out at Everett on October 14, 1971, and delivered to the customer on March 9, 1972. The aircraft could carry three times the weight of cargo than the 707. During the 1970s and 1980s, engine power continued to increase and so did the all-up weights of the 747, permitting even greater cargo payloads to be carried. The -300 series was never produced in freighter form, though the -300M combi proved quite popular. However, after a number of surplus -300 aircraft became available during the late 1990s, Boeing announced a -300SF conversion programme on May 31, 2000. Atlas Air was the first customer with an order for three aircraft, and these have now been delivered, the first arriving on October 17, 2000, following modification at Boeing's plant in Wichita, Kansas.

The arrival of the 747-400 in the late 1980s led to the addition of the -400F in 1989. Compared to the -200F, it can carry 26 more tons of cargo for a further 1,380 miles (2,220km) with a 12% improvement in fuel consumption. It will be of little surprise to hear that the -400F has been a huge success, with 98 orders by August 2001 as well as 63 orders for -400M combis.

Images of all marks of freighters can be found throughout the relevant type chapters and Airlines chapter.

Right: Iran Air now operates a single -200F, though there are many other operators with only a few freighters on their books. However, other dedicated cargo carriers, such as UPS and Cargolux, have significant numbers and fly an extensive network of routes transporting cargo worldwide. (Schiphol Group)

Centre right: Another freighter variant was the -200C convertible. This is the first example, originally registered as N747WA (c/n 20651) and delivered to World Airways on April 27, 1973. It was leased to Pan Am in October 1974 for a five-year period and is currently registered to Wilmington Trust Co as N471EV. Only 13 -200Cs were sold, a surprisingly small number since it offered complete flexibility, being adaptable to all-passenger or all-cargo configurations or a combination of the two. (Boeing)

Left: The work involved in converting a standard passenger 747 into a freighter is far more complex than simply removing the seats and fitting a couple of cargo doors. The whole main deck floor must be reinforced to take the extra payload weight, and numerous other alterations are necessary. (Boeing)

Bottom left: The long and cavernous main cargo deck of a Cathay Pacific 747-467F demonstrates the huge carrying potential of the Jumbo freighter. (Airliner World – Tony Dixon)

Bottom right: The 747-400F is the latest and most capable version of the 747 Freighter. It was made available from 1989 and has seen worldwide sales to a number of customers. (Cargolux)

Bottom far right: As well as the hinged front door, most cargo aircraft have the side cargo door fitted. This one has been installed in a UPS 747-200F passenger conversion by IAI/Bedek Aviation Group of Israel. (IAI)

By the mid 1980s, the 747 was rapidly approaching its 20th year and its age was beginning to show. Indeed, the poor take-up of the -300 was a clear indication to Boeing that the airlines were becoming more particular and with the advent of the McDonnell Douglas MD-11 and Airbus A330/340 family, competition was becoming fierce. What was needed was a complete update of the 747, not only to provide more range and capacity, but also to incorporate the latest developments in technology.

Boeing announced the launch of the 747-400 in May 1985 and it undertook a massive upgrade of the basic 747 design. The company originally intended only limited changes to the cockpit, but pressure from the airlines forced it to radically overhaul this area with advanced technology. The result is a two-crew cockpit, the flight engineer's position being rendered obsolete by advanced electronic flight instrumentation system (EFIS) flat screen displays (a total of six) and other new technology. The level of automation of basic and even complex tasks helped to vastly simplify procedures and to reduce the number of gauges and switches from 971 on the earliest 747s to just 365 in the -400. Fuel management became fully automatic and the aircraft now had the ability to perform automatic landings in bad weather. Other advanced equipment fitted included a datalink, collision avoidance equipment, windshear warning, full authority digital engine control (FADEC) and 4D navigation with the aid of a Honeywell (Sperry)

747-400 SPECIFICATIONS	
Wingspan	211ft 5in (64.44m)
Length	231ft 10in (70.66m)
Height	63ft 5in (19.5m)
Wing area	5,825sq ft (541.16m²)
Weight empty	391,000lb (177,400kg)
Weight maximum	870,000lb (394,630kg)
Fuel capacity	57,200 US gals (215,745 litres)
Cruising speed	612mph (985km/h)
Ceiling	45,000ft (13,700m)
Range	8,400 miles (13,500km)
Passenger capacity	Up to 496 typically, maximum of 630
Powerplants choice of	4 x Pratt & Whitney PW4056
	4 x General Electric CF6-80C2B1F
	4 x Rolls-Royce RB211-524G/H

flight management computer system (FMCS). As well as course plotting using its inertial navigation system, the FMCS can also monitor and analyse fuel burn statistics to predict time to altitude at waypoints (4D), thus greatly assisting both the flight crew and air traffic control.

The rest of the airframe was also treated to a series of improvements, especially with the use of new lightweight materials, such as alloys or composites, which offered more strength, resistance to corrosion and an improved

Right: Air France 747-428 F-GITA (c/n 24969) gets airborne at Paine Field, Everett, Washington, on February 28, 1991, marking delivery of the first of the new -400 series to the French carrier. (Boeing)

747–400 OPERATORS

Abu Dhabi Government	Government
Air Canada	KLM Royal Dutch Airlines
Air China	Korean Air
Air France	Kuwait Airways
Air India	Lufthansa
Air Namibia	Malaysian Airline System
Air New Zealand	
All Nippon Airways	Mandarin Airlines
Ansett Australia	Northwest Airlines
Asiana Airlines	Oman Government
Atlas Air	Philippine Airlines
British Airways	Polar Air Cargo
Brunei Government	Qantas
Canadian Airlines International	Royal Air Maroc
	Saudi Arabian Airlines
Cargolux	Singapore Airlines
Cathay Pacific Airways	South African Airways
	Thai Airways International
China Airlines	
El Al	Union de Transports Aeriens
Emirates SkyCargo	
Eva Airways	United Air Lines
Garuda Indonesian Airways	United States Air Force
	Varig
Japan Air Lines	Virgin Atlantic Airways
Japan Air System	
Japanese	

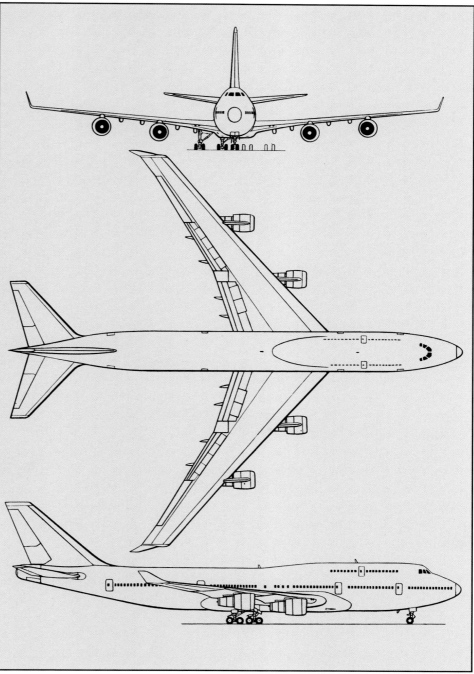

Left: The first -400 was c/n 23719, a 747-451 destined for Northwest Airlines as N611US but initially was used for flight testing by Boeing. It was joined by three other development aircraft, one powered by Pratt & Whitney engines, one by General Electric and another by Rolls-Royce powerplants. Of particular interest was a test flight undertaken on May 26, 1988, which has gone into the record books as the longest engineering test flight in commercial aviation history, lasting over 14 hours to test the aircraft's cruise performance. (Boeing)

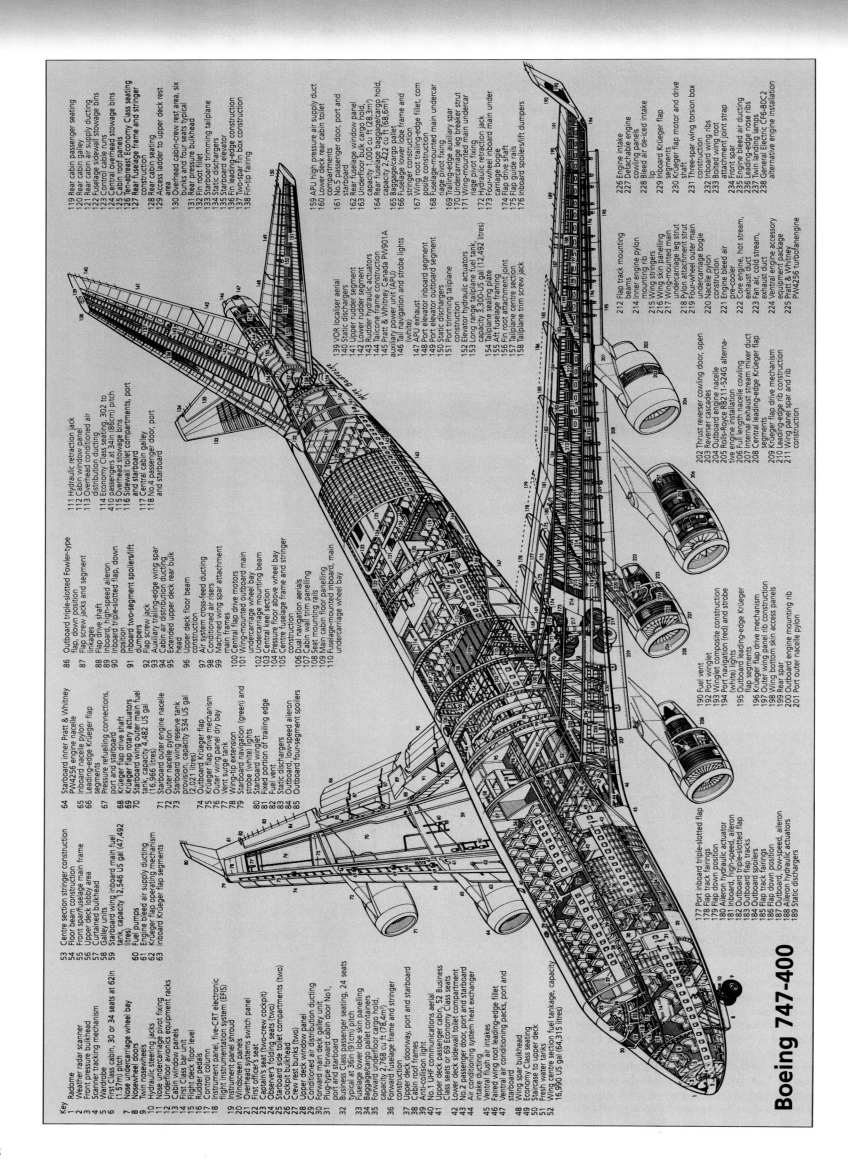

Boeing 747-400

Key
1 Radome
2 Weather radar scanner
3 Front pressure bulkhead
4 Scanner tracking mechanism
5 Wardrobe
6 First Class cabin, 30 or 34 seats at 62in (1.57m) pitch
7 Nose undercarriage wheel bay
8 Nosewheel doors
9 Twin nosewheels
10 Hydraulic steering jacks
11 Nose undercarriage pivot fixing
12 Underfloor avionics equipment racks
13 Cabin window panels
14 First Class bar unit
15 Flight deck floor level
16 Rudder pedals
17 Control column
18 Instrument panel, five-CRT electronic flight instrumentation system (EFIS)
19 Instrument panel shroud
20 Windscreen panels
21 Overhead systems switch panel
22 First officer's seat
23 Captain's seat (two-crew cockpit)
24 Observer's folding seats (two)
25 Starboard side toilet compartments (two)
26 Cockpit bulkhead
27 Crew rest bunks (two)
28 Upper deck window panel
29 Conditioned air distribution ducting
30 Forward main deck galley unit
31 Plug-type forward cabin door No.1, port and starboard
32 Business Class passenger seating, 24 seats typical at 36in (91cm) pitch
33 Fuselage lower lobe skin panelling
34 Baggage/cargo pallet containers
35 Forward underfloor cargo hold, capacity 2,768 cu ft (78.4m³)
36 Forward fuselage frame and stringer construction
37 Upper deck doorway, port and starboard
38 Cabin roof frames
39 Anti-collision light
40 No.1 UHF communications aerial
41 Upper deck passenger cabin, 52 Business Class seats or 69 Economy Class seats
42 Lower deck sidewall toilet compartment
43 No.2 passenger door, port and starboard
44 Air conditioning system heat exchanger intake ducting
45 Ventral flush air intakes
46 Faired wing root leading-edge fillet
47 Ventral air conditioning packs, port and starboard
48 Wing spar bulkhead
49 Economy Class seating
50 Staircase to upper deck
51 Fresh water tanks
52 Wing centre section fuel tankage, capacity 16,990 US gal (64,315 litres)
53 Centre section stringer construction
54 Floor beam construction
55 Front spar/fuselage main frame
56 Upper deck lobby area
57 Curtained bulkhead
58 Galley units
59 Starboard wing inboard main fuel tank, capacity 12,546 US gal (47,492 litres)
60 Fuel pumps
61 Engine bleed air supply ducting
62 Krueger flap operating mechanism
63 Inboard Krueger flap segments
64 Starboard inner Pratt & Whitney PW4256 engine nacelle
65 Inboard nacelle pylon
66 Leading-edge Krueger flap segments
67 Pressure refuelling connections, port and starboard
68 Krueger flap drive shaft
69 Krueger flap rotary actuators
70 Starboard wing outer main fuel tank, capacity 4,482 US gal (16,966 litres)
71 Starboard outer engine nacelle
72 Outer nacelle pylon
73 Starboard wing reserve tank provision, capacity 534 US gal (2,021 litres)
74 Outboard Krueger flap
75 Krueger flap drive mechanism
76 Outer wing panel dry bay
77 Vent surge tank
78 Wing-tip extension
79 Starboard navigation (green) and strobe (white) lights
80 Starboard winglet
81 Fixed portion of trailing edge
82 Fuel vent
83 Static dischargers
84 Outboard, low-speed aileron
85 Outboard four-segment spoilers
86 Outboard triple-slotted Fowler-type flap, down position
87 Flap screw jacks and segment linkages
88 Flap drive shaft
89 Inboard, high-speed aileron
90 Inboard triple-slotted flap, down position
91 Inboard two-segment spoilers/lift dumpers
92 Flap screw jack
93 Auxiliary trailing-edge wing spar
94 Cabin air distribution ducting
95 Extended upper deck rear bulkhead
96 Upper deck floor beam construction
97 Air system cross-feed ducting
98 Conditioned air risers
99 Machined wing spar attachment main frames
100 Central flap drive motors
101 Wing-mounted outboard main undercarriage wheel bay
102 Undercarriage mounting beam
103 Central keel section
104 Pressure floor above wheel bay
105 Centre fuselage frame and stringer construction
106 Dual navigation aerials
107 Cabin wall trim panelling
108 Seat mounting rails
109 Main cabin floor panelling
110 Fuselage-mounted inboard, main undercarriage wheel bay
111 Hydraulic retraction jack
112 Cabin window panel
113 Overhead conditioned air distribution ducting
114 Economy Class seating, 302 to 410 passengers at 34in (86cm) pitch
115 Overhead stowage bins
116 Sidewall toilet compartments, port and starboard
117 Central cabin galley
118 No.4 passenger door, port and starboard
119 Rear cabin passenger seating
120 Rear cabin galley
121 Rear cabin air supply ducting
122 Fuselage sidewall stowage bins
123 Control cable runs
124 Central overhead stowage bins
125 Cabin roof panels
126 Ten-abreast Economy Class seating
127 Rear fuselage frame and stringer construction
128 Rear cabin seating
129 Access ladder to upper deck rest area
130 Overhead cabin-crew rest area, six bunks and four seats typical
131 Rear pressure bulkhead
132 Rear fin root fillet
133 Starboard trimming tailplane
134 Static dischargers
135 Starboard elevator
136 Fin leading-edge construction
137 Two-spar fin box construction
138 Fin-tip fairing
139 VOR localiser aerial
140 Static dischargers
141 Upper rudder segment
142 Lower rudder segment
143 Rudder hydraulic actuators
144 Tailcone frame construction
145 Pratt & Whitney Canada PW901A auxiliary power unit (APU)
146 Tail navigation and strobe lights (white)
147 APU exhaust
148 Port elevator inboard segment
149 Port elevator outboard segment
150 Static dischargers
151 Port trimming tailplane construction
152 Elevator hydraulic actuators
153 Long range tailplane fuel tank, capacity 3,300-US gal (12,492 litres)
154 Aft fuselage framing
155 Tailplane sealing plate
156 Fin root attachment joint
157 Tailplane centre section
158 Tailplane trim screw jack
159 APU high pressure air supply duct
160 Lower deck rear cabin toilet compartments
161 No.5 passenger door, port and starboard
162 Rear fuselage window panel
163 Underfloor bulk cargo hold, capacity 1,000 cu ft (28.3m³)
164 Rear fuselage baggage/cargo hold, capacity 2,422 cu ft (68.6m³)
165 Baggage/cargo pallet
166 Fuselage lower lobe frame and stringer construction
167 Wing root trailing-edge fillet, composite construction
168 Fuselage-mounted main undercarriage pivot fixing
169 Trailing-edge auxiliary spar
170 Undercarriage leg breaker strut
171 Wing-mounted main undercarriage pivot fixing
172 Hydraulic retraction jack
173 Four-wheel outer main undercarriage bogie
174 Four-wheel inboard main under carriage bogie
175 Flap guide rails
176 Inboard spoilers/lift dumpers
177 Port inboard triple-slotted flap
178 Flap track fairings
179 Flap down position
180 Aileron hydraulic actuator
181 Inboard, high-speed, aileron
182 Outboard triple-slotted flap
183 Outboard flap tracks
184 Outboard spoilers
185 Flap track fairings
186 Flap down position
187 Outboard, low-speed, aileron
188 Aileron hydraulic actuators
189 Static dischargers
190 Fuel vent
191 Winglet
192 Fuel tank fairings
193 Winglet composite construction
194 Port navigation (red) and strobe (white) lights
195 Outboard leading-edge Krüger flap segments
196 Krüger flap drive mechanism
197 Outer wing panel rib construction
198 Wing bottom skin access panels
199 Rear spar
200 Outboard engine mounting rib
201 Port outer nacelle pylon
202 Thrust reverser cowling door, open
203 Reverser cascades
204 Outboard engine nacelle
205 Rolls-Royce RB211-524G alternative engine installation
206 Full length nacelle cowling
207 Internal exhaust stream mixer duct
208 Central leading-edge Krüger flap segments
209 Krüger flap drive mechanism
210 Leading-edge rib construction
211 Wing panel spar and rib construction
212 Flap track mounting beams
213 Inner engine pylon
214 Inboard engine nacelle
215 Wing stringers
216 Wing skin panelling
217 Wing-mounted main undercarriage leg strut
218 Pylon attachment strut
219 Four-wheel outer main undercarriage bogie
220 Nacelle pylon construction
221 Engine bleed air pre-cooler
222 Core engine, hot stream, exhaust duct
223 Fan air, cold stream, exhaust duct
224 Ventral engine accessory equipment package
225 Pratt & Whitney PW4256 turbofan engine
226 Engine intake
227 Detachable engine cowling panels
228 Bleed air de-iced intake lip
229 Inboard Krüger flap
230 Krüger flap motor and drive shaft
231 Three-spar wing torsion box construction
232 Inboard wing ribs
233 Bolted wing root attachment joint strap
234 Front spar
235 Engine bleed air ducting
236 Leading-edge nose ribs
237 Twin landing lamps
238 General Electric CF6-80C2 alternative engine installation

Below: Boeing 747-4F6 N752PR (c/n 27262) of Philippines Airlines at Hong Kong's old Kai Tak airport on October 1, 1995. This aircraft was delivered to the carrier on December 21, 1993. (Robbie Shaw)

Bottom: The vast majority of the -400s so far delivered by Boeing have remained with the original operator. Garuda Indonesia Airways 747-4U3 PK-GSH (c/n 25705) is no exception to this rule, and is seen here at Frankfurt in June 1999. (Airliner World collection)

fatigue life. But the weight-saving factor was the most critical in helping to boost the aircraft's range. For example, the original steel brakes were replaced by BFGoodrich carbon examples, instantly saving 1,800lb (816kg). The wingspan was increased to 211ft 5in (64.44m) and the wings were fitted with graphite winglets to improve aerodynamic performance when in high altitude cruise. The 747-400D (Domestic) version for the Japanese high-density routes does not have the winglets since its short-haul flights would see no benefit. This version can seat up to 568 economy passengers, the largest number available on any current airliner.

Inside the passenger cabin another revolution was under way. New lightweight fire-resistant materials were used and a very flexible layout enabled the aircraft to be configured in hundreds of different ways to suit individual airline requirements. The overhead stowage bins were doubled in capacity and new side panels and ceilings, plus re-designs of galleys, toilets, air conditioning and cabin services, all helped to offer the passenger a much improved experience.

More powerful engines were once again required and all three of the major engine manufacturers have produced powerplants for the aircraft in the 60,000lb (270kN) thrust range. All of these have delivered improved fuel burn and economy over older engines, as well as providing even higher reliability and less maintenance. Through the increase in engine power, maximum take-off weight for the -400 varies from 800,000lb (362,880kg) to 870,000lb (394,632kg) with a range of up to 8,400 miles (13,500km). Fuel capacity was increased with the addition of 3,300 US gal of tank space in the horizontal tail and the combination of all of these measures meant the 747-400 had the range to fly non-stop on routes such as London to Singapore, eliminating the need for an intermediate fuel stop.

As well as the -400D, there are also combi and freighter versions of the -400 and all versions have enjoyed considerable sales. The increase in cargo capacity has not been lost on the dedicated cargo carriers: the -400 can carry 124 tons of freight, 26 tons more than the -200F. One noticeable difference is the return to the shorter upper deck on the -400F, there being no need for the upper deck capacity of the passenger version.

The complexities of revamping an old design led to delays and Boeing learned much from the process and implemented new procedures for the new 777 programme. One area that impacted on design, parts supply and production was the massive range of interior layouts and specifications offered to the airlines. These were eventu-

ally streamlined to a limited number of configurations to ease the situation.

The -400 was an instant success and enjoyed huge early orders, numbering 117 by the time of the roll out of the first aircraft, a 747-451 (c/n 23719, registration N661US) for Northwest Airlines, on January 26, 1988. Maiden flight took place on April 29 that year and by June, orders had risen to 146. After FAA certification on January 9, 1989, the -400 entered service in early 1989. By December 2001, a total of 627 747-400s had been ordered, making it by far the most successful 747 variant.

Right: Thai Airways International operates 14 CF6-80-powered 747-4D7s, among them HS-TGM (c/n 27093), seen here adorned with special markings to mark the Thai King's 72nd birthday. The -400 series has proved immensely popular in the Asia region, and the most recent orders for the type have come from here. (Airliner World – Tony Dixon)

Below: Saudi Arabian Airlines took delivery of 747-468 HZ-AIW (c/n 28340) on February 13, 1998. The aircraft first flew on January 28, 1998, and is seen here departing from Manchester on March 27, 2000. (Nigel Prevett)

Opposite page, bottom: KLM has operated the -200, -300 and -400 versions of the Jumbo, a great many of these as the combi variant. The airline has received 16 of 19 747-406M combis and five standard 747-406s from Boeing since 1990. Here 747-406 PH-BFG (c/n 24517) gets underway for another long-haul flight from the airline's home at Amsterdam Schiphol, in the Netherlands. (Robbie Shaw)

Right: Cargolux is Europe's largest cargo airline and operates a fleet of 747-200 and -400 freighters. The company started life in March 1970 using Canadair CL44J turboprops, though today the -400F offers far greater payload capacity. The -400F was introduced by the airline in 1993 and is used on routes to Asia, South Africa and the USA. One of the more recent deliveries to the airline is 747-4R7F LX-RCV (c/n 30400) seen here at Johannesburg, South Africa, in September 2000. (Airliner World – Tony Dixon)

Right: Kuwait Airways operates a single 747-469M, 9K-ADE (c/n 27338), seen here departing on delivery to the customer at Paine Field, Everett, on November 29, 1994. (Boeing)

Below: A United Air Lines 747-422 during its 40° turn to line up on runway 13 at Kai Tak airport in Hong Kong. The airline has since revised its livery and the airport has closed, having been replaced by the new Chek Lap Kok airport. (Airliner World – Malcolm English)

Left: Northwest Airlines applied this special scheme to 747-451 N670US (c/n 24225) in 1997 to celebrate 50 years of transpacific services between the USA and Asia. What makes the photo interesting is that it was taken at Amsterdam Schiphol Airport. This aircraft, for obvious reasons, was mostly confined to Pacific routes. (Northwest Airlines)

Left: A number of Asian operators experienced financial difficulties during the late 1990s due to an economic slump in the region. As a result, a number of new build 747-400s were not taken up by some airlines. Among those affected was Asiana Airlines, which should have taken delivery of this 747-48E (c/n 28552) in mid-1998. However, it went straight into desert storage at Marana, Arizona, in June 1998, was later sold to General Electric Capital Aviation Services on June 18, 1999, and was leased to Asiana Airlines on the same date. It is seen here departing from Los Angeles International Airport in February 2000. (Robbie Shaw)

Left: British Airways is the largest single operator of the -400, having ordered 57 Rolls-Royce RB211-524 powered examples. The airline accelerated the retirement of its final -200 series aircraft in October 2001 and now only operates the -400 variant. One of the early 747-436s to be delivered was G-BNLD (c/n 23911) *City of Belfast*, seen here at London Gatwick in October 1997. (Robbie Shaw)

Above: Canadian Airlines International 747-475 C-FBCA (c/n 25422) on approach to Kai Tak airport in Hong Kong. The airline operated four CF6-80-powered -475s, this example bearing the name *G W Grant McConanchie*. (Robbie Shaw)

Right: 747-437 VT-ESO (c/n 27165), the 1009th 747 built climbs away from Bombay in February 2001. Air India has six Pratt & Whitney PW4056 -400s, the airline also operates the -200 and -300 series Jumbos. (Airliner World – Alan Warnes)

Right: EVA Airways has ordered a total of 18 -400s, comprising seven -400s, three -400Fs and eight -400Ms. Illustrated is N406EV (c/n 27898), a 747-45E SCD at Kai Tak in November 1997. This aircraft was delivered to the airline on January 11, 1995, but sold to Hokkaido Takushoko Bank on the same day and immediately leased back to Eva Airways. It was re-registered as B-18407 with the operator in July 1999. (Robbie Shaw)

Left: Brazilian carrier Varig leased three -400s during the early 1990s for use on its long-haul routes. This example, PP-VPI (c/n 24896), was delivered to the airline on May 31, 1991, though it was owned by International Lease Finance Corporation (ILFC). Varig returned it, along with the other two examples, c/ns 24956 and 24957, during 1994. This aircraft is currently leased to Air New Zealand as ZK-SUH. (Boeing)

Bottom left: Virgin Atlantic Airways currently operates both -200 classic and -400 Jumbos. It has 11 -400s at present, a mix of new and leased aircraft. Illustrated is 747-41R G-VAST (c/n 28757), about to land at Los Angeles in February 1998. (Robbie Shaw)

Top right: Two colourful Jumbos pass by at London Heathrow in November 1999, a Singapore Airlines -400 and a South African Airways -200. This 747-412, 9V-SPL (c/n 26557), is one of two to wear this attractive scheme and was delivered to the airline on January 30, 1997. The other aircraft, 9V-SPK (c/n28023), was involved in a tragic take-off accident at Taipei Chiang Kai-Shek International Airport, Taiwan, on October 31, 2000. (Peter Cooper)

Right: Air New Zealand 747-419 ZK-NBT (c/n 24855) at London Gatwick in September 1993, wearing the airline's old colours. The airline currently has eight -400 series 747s, four purchased from Boeing and the remaining four leased or bought from other operators. (Robbie Shaw)

Right: Brand-new Polar Air Cargo 747-46NF N450PA (c/n 30808) undergoing last-minute checks at Everett on October 3, 2000, before being delivered to the customer on October 16. The aircraft is the first of five examples being leased from GECAS. (Airliner World – Tony Dixon)

Above: Malaysian Airline Systems 747-4H6 9M-MPN (c/n 28429), one of 23 ordered by the Asian operator. So far 18 have been delivered, 16 -4H6s and two -4H6Ms: a further five Pratt & Whitney powered -4H6s remain outstanding. (Malaysian Airline Systems)

Top right: Hong Kong-based Cathay Pacific is a prolific 747 operator and has a thriving cargo operation. Its 747-467F B-HUH (c/n 27175) climbs out from East Midlands airport in the UK in February 2001. It is one of three freighters currently with the airline: two more are on order. (Airliner World – Tony Dixon)

Upper left: This aircraft was another casualty of the Asian economic crisis of the late 1990s. It was destined for Philippines Airlines but was not taken up by the airline. Instead it went into store at Marana, Arizona, before being delivered to South African Airways as ZS-SBS (c/n 28960) on December 31, 1998. (Airliner World – Tony Dixon)

Left: Lufthansa 747-430M combi D-ABTH (c/n 2047) banks past the famous chequerboard onto the final approach at Hong Kong's Kai Tak airport on November 11, 1994. The German airline currently operates 26 -400 series Jumbos including seven combis. It also has a further three -400s on order. (Robbie Shaw)

Right: Korean Air was one of the many Asian airlines to feel the effects of the 1990s Asian economic crisis. This aircraft, 747-4B5 HL7404 (c/n 26409) was initially stored at Marana, Arizona, in August 1998 before being delivered to the airline at the end of December that year. Complex financial arrangements between Boeing and the operator have enabled it to restructure its payment so as to maintain its considerable fleet of aircraft, most of which are Boeing products. HL7404 is seen departing from Los Angeles bound for Korea in February 2000. (Robbie Shaw)

Lower right: One of the earlier -400 series to be delivered was this 747-438 (VH-OJB (c/n 24373) which arrived with the Australian carrier Qantas on September 15, 1989. In 1994 it received this Aboriginal design paint scheme depicting tales of journeys taken by spirit ancestors, and the name *Wunala Dreaming*. The airline instigated a $250 million investment programme for its -400s in 1998 which included fitting luxurious fully-reclining sleeper seats in First Class, electronically operated 'Dreamtime' seats with five-way touch pad controls in Business Class, and new technology Economy Class seats. Interior decor and galleys were also refurbished. (Airliner World collection)

Left: The Japanese Air Self Defence Force is currently the only military operator of the -400. It has two 747-47Cs, 20-1101 and 20-1102 (c/ns 24730 & 24731), both of which were delivered to the operator on April 1, 1992, after originally being handed over to the Japanese Government on September 17, 1991 and November 18, 1991 respectively. The US Air Force has taken delivery of the first of seven -400F airframes for conversion to an airborne laser platform. Conversion work is currently underway at Wichita, Kansas. (Robbie Shaw)

Right: Recently delivered to Atlas Air is this 747-47UF N409MC (c/n 30558). The aircraft is seen at Anchorage, Alaska, and is one of 16 ordered by the cargo operator. More recently it was leased by Alitalia. (Robbie Shaw)

Left: China Airlines 747-412 3B-SMC (c/n 24063) comes in to land at Kai Tak, Hong Kong, on November 15, 1994. This aircraft was delivered to Singapore Airlines on July 11, 1989, and leased to China Airlines as 3B-SMC on June 1, 1994, for a three-year period. Although operated by the Taiwan-based airline, it was registered in Mauritius. (Robbie Shaw)

Right: Air China 747-4J6 B-2445 (c/n 25882) drops down over the Hong Kong high-rise in November 1996. The aircraft is one of 14 owned by the airline, having been delivered on February 25, 1994. All the operator's aircraft are powered by Pratt & Whitney PW4056 engines; the fleet comprising six -400s and eight -400Ms. (Airliner World – Malcolm English)

Left: Mandarin Airlines sole 747-409, B-16801 (c/n 27965), at Hong Kong Kai Tak on November 22, 1997. The aircraft is powered by Pratt & Whitney PW4056 engines and was delivered to the airline on June 14, 1995. (Nigel Prevett)

Above: The world's largest 747 operator is Japan Air Lines, which has ordered a total of 45 of the digital flight deck equipped 747-400 while continuing to operate a significant number of older variants. JAL's 747-446 JA8902 (c/n 26344) climbs out of Kansai, Japan, on April 27, 1998. (Robbie Shaw)

Left: Boeing 747-4B3 F-GEXA (c/n 24154) was handed over to UTA on July 16, 1991, but the airline merged with Air France in December 1992 and it is seen here swooping into Kai Tak airport, Hong Kong on April 23, 1998, wearing special markings for the 1998 World Cup. (Robbie Shaw)

Left: Johannesburg is the setting for Singapore Airlines' 747-412F 9V-SFA (c/n 26563) as it departs on another cargo flight in September 2000. Note the curvature in the wings, caused by the huge amount of lift they generate at take-off with the help of the leading edge Krüeger flaps and the triple-slotted trailing edge flaps. (Airliner World – Tony Dixon)

Upper right: The General Electric CF6-80C2 hi-bypass turbofan engine was introduced for the -200 series and has been available in increasingly-powerful versions for all subsequent 747 variants. (General Electric)

Bottom right: The original Pratt & Whitney JT9D engines encountered considerable development problems, but these were eventually overcome to provide a reliable and efficient powerplant.

Below: The Rolls-Royce RB211 family of engines has proved to be hugely successful and has benefited from the company's work on its Trent series of engines. Latest RB211s include the advanced core from the Trent and offer improved performance, lower fuel consumption and reduced maintenance over earlier models. (Rolls-Royce)

The Boeing 747 required an entirely new and more powerful engine if the project was to succeed. General Electric was developing the TF-39 for the C-5 Galaxy and although this was of sufficient power for the 747, it was being developed for the slower C-5 transport aircraft and consequently was not suitable for the 747. GE did not have the resources at the time to develop the engine for the 747 and so Pratt & Whitney stepped in with its own design, the JT9D. This was duly selected, but the revolutionary engine encountered a host of teething problems which caused considerable delay to the 747 programme in its first years. It is fascinating to reflect that each JT9D-3 produced 43,500lb (193.48kN) of thrust – as much power as all four turbojets fitted to the early model 707s. The engine was huge, the front fan measuring 8ft (2.4m) in diameter, but some areas needed redesign by Pratt & Whitney after bending stresses in the turbine casing were encountered during take-off, something which was to take considerable effort before it was finally eliminated. To assist in the engine's development, one was fitted to the starboard inner pylon of a B-52E (56-0636) bomber for flight trials in 1968, and it was during these tests that many of the initial problems were identified.

Fortunately, the difficulties associated with such a new and complex engine were progressively addressed and the engine achieved sustained reliability. But no sooner had these difficulties been overcome than Pratt & Whitney began to receive requests for more powerful variants as the projected weight of the evolving 747 increased. These were duly satisfied, with the basic JT9D being developed

through a series of versions until it was replaced by the PW4056 for the 747-400.

Once General Electric had completed its work with the military TF-39, it continued development of a commercial derivative. Boeing decided to market the 747 with a choice of engines, the P&W JT9D and the GE CF6-50D/E. The GE engine was promising 51,000lb (226.48kN) of thrust with a 5% reduction in fuel consumption, so offering both performance and range advantages. Equally important was the fact that this engine was more attractive to the military and was also available for the latest Airbus A300 and McDonnell Douglas DC-10 aircraft. The GE engines were air tested aboard the developmental 747 (N7470) during June 1973 and following 130 hours of flight testing the engine received full certification in January 1974. The first customer was the USAF, with the CF6 being fitted to the third of its E-4 command post aircraft. The first commercial sale was to the Dutch national airline KLM, which ordered the engine for its 747-200s, the first (PH-BUA) being delivered on January 26, 1971. It was not long before other airlines also opted for the GE powerplant.

Not to be outdone, Rolls-Royce was also developing a hi-bypass turbofan engine, the RB211. Although originally intended for the Lockheed TriStar, the RB211 offered suitable thrust for the 747 and it was selected by British Airways and other airlines for all variants of the 747 including the SP.

From the early and troubled days of the original JT9D, the power output available to the 747 has risen

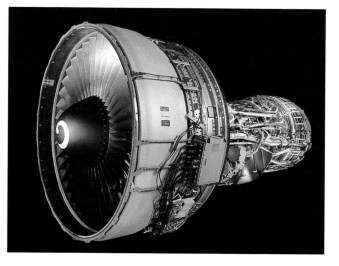

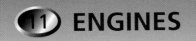

747 ENGINE CHOICES

Manufacturer/powerplant	Thrust rating		Manufacturer/powerplant	Thrust rating
747-100			**747-200**	
P&W JT9D-1 (prototype)	42,000lb (186.81kN)		GE CF6-50E2	52,500lb (233.52kN)
P&W JT9D-3	43,500lb (193.48kN)		GE CF6-80C281	56,700lb (252.20kN)
P&W JT9D-3AW	45,000lb (200.16kN)		GE CF6-80C2B1	56,750lb (252.42kN)
P&W JT9D-7 (derated)*	34,500lb (153.45kN)		RR RB211-524B2	50,100lb (222.84kN)
P&W JT9D-7	45,500lb (202.38kN)		RR RB211-524C2	51,600lb (229.5kN)
P&W JT9D-7A	46,950lb (208.83kN)		RR RB211-524D4	53,110lb (236.25kN)
P&W JT9D-7AW	48,570lb (216kN)			
P&W JT9D-7F	48,000lb (213.50kN)		**747-300**	
P&W JT9D-7J	50,000lb (222.40kN)		P&W JT9D-7R4G2	54,750lb (243.52kN)
P&W JT9D-9W	47,900lb (213.05kN)		GE CF6-80C2B1	55,640lb (247.48kN)
GE CF6-50E2	52,500lb (233.52kN)		RR RB211-524D4	53,000lb (235.74kN)
GE CF6-45A	46,500lb (206.83kN)			
RR RB211-524B2	50,100lb (222.84kN)		**747-400**	
RR RB211-524C	51,000lb (226.48kN)		P&W PW4056	56,000lb (249.08kN)
*Used on early SR models			P&W PW4060	60,000lb (266.88kN)
			P&W PW4062	62,000lb (275.77kN)
747SP			GE CF6-80C2B1F	56,900lb (253.09kN)
P&W JT9D-7A	46,950lb (208.83kN)		GE CF6-80C2B1F1/-80C2B7F	61,500lb (273.55kN)
P&W JT9D-7AW	48,570lb (216kN)		RR RB211-524G	58,000lb (257.98kN)
GE CF6-45A2	46,500lb (206.83kN)		RR RB211-524H	60,600lb (269.54kN)
RR RB211-524B2	50,100lb (222.84kN)			
RR RB211-524C2	51,600lb (229.5kN)		**747-400ER**	
RR RB211-524D4 (derated)	51,000lb (226.48kN)		P&W PW4062	63,300lb (281.55kN)
			GE CF6-80C2B5F	61,100lb (271.77kN)
747-200			RR RB211-524H6-T-19	59,500lb (264.65kN)
P&W JT9D-7AW	48,570lb (216kN)			
P&W JT9D-7FW	50,000lb (222.40kN)		**747X**	
P&W JT9D-7R4G2	54,750lb (243.52kN)		Engine Alliance GP7168	68,000lb (302.46kN)
P&W JT9D-7R4H	56,000lb (249.08kN)		RR Trent 600	68,000lb - 72,000lb (302.46kN - 320kN)

from 41,000lb (182.36kN) to over 60,000lb (266.88kN) today, an increase which has been accompanied by huge improvements in fuel efficiency and reliability. All three manufacturers have continued to improve their products to include the very latest technology and today in-flight engine shut downs are almost unheard of. Rolls-Royce now utilises the advanced core of its Trent series engines within the latest RB211 range and this

has both benefited fuel efficiency and power output. While Boeing was considering the 747X models, the engine manufacturers were also having to keep pace with even more refined products. Both the Engine Alliance and Rolls-Royce tabled proposals for powering the aircraft and Rolls Royce announced the formal launch of the Trent 600 for the 747X on February 13, 2001.

Far left: Early 747s had the ability to carry a spare engine for transit purposes in a special fifth pod mounted under the inner port wing. Illustrated is TWA 747-257B N303TW (c/n 20116) with the fifth pod attached. This aircraft was originally sold to Swissair, but was bought by TWA in 1985. (Robbie Shaw)

Left: The Pratt & Whitney PW4056 superseded the JT9D for the 747-400 series and is also available in 4060 and 4062 versions, offering even more power. (Pratt & Whitney)

Considering that the 747 was aimed at the long-haul market it is probably surprising to see, through the individual type operators' lists, just how many airlines have flown the big airliner. Boeing initially thought that only the major operators would have either the requirement or the resources to utilise the aircraft. What actually happened was that many smaller airlines ordered limited numbers so as to expand into the rapidly-growing long-haul market, and other airlines later snapped up low-cost second hand aircraft as a cheaper way of generating more revenue once the type was established.

It is interesting to compare the operator tables for the -200 and -400. The -400 has been built in much larger numbers, yet it has so far been operated by considerably fewer airlines. This is because most of the smaller operators are quite content to continue to use their -200 or -300 models while the larger airlines can justify the expenditure on the newer and more capable -400. In fact, since its entry into service in 1989, the -400 has increasingly replaced older models with major airlines such as British Airways and United Airlines, two of the largest -400 operators. Over the 32 years the Boeing 747 has been in service, many airlines have come and gone while others have merged to form even larger concerns, and it is this latter development, particularly in North America, that has influenced purchase trends for new aircraft. The number of leasing companies has proliferated in recent years and a considerable number of operators are taking this route to acquire aircraft. It is a reasonably safe assumption that the overall number of 747 operators will not increase significantly from where it is now, especially after the events of September 11, 2001.. Airlines are constantly reviewing their costs and equipment, and with modern-day customer demand leaning more towards long distance point-to-point services, aircraft such as the long range 767 and 777 models, or the Airbus A330/340, are seeing increasing popularity. Routes with heavy passenger loadings will continue to need an aircraft the size of the 747, or maybe the Airbus A380, and so the future of the 747 with airlines on such routes is assured.

Below: Pan American Airways was the launch customer for the Boeing 747-100 when it placed the first order for 25 aircraft in 1966. Sadly, this airline is no longer with us, but without the pioneering and risk-taking nature of its boss, Juan Trippe, the giant airliner might have remained a drawing board fantasy. (Boeing)

CURRENT BOEING 747 OPERATORS

Operator	Type	Aircraft	Operator	Type	Aircraft	Operator	Type	Aircraft
Abu Dhabi Government	SP	1	Bahrain Government	SP	1		-300	3
	-400	1	British Airways	-400	56	Iran Air	-100B	1
Aerolineas Argentinas	-200B	7		-400F	1		-200F	1
Aeromar Airlines	-200B	1	Brunei Government	-400	1		-200B SCD	2
Air Algerie	-200B	1	Cargo Air Lines	-200C	2		SP	4
Air Atlanta Iceland	-200B	5	Cargolux	-400F	11	Iranian Air Force	-100 SCD	5
Air Canada	-400	4	Cathay Pacific Airways	-200F	3	Iraqi Airways	SP	1
	-400 SCD	4		-200B SCD	1	Japan Air Lines	-100	2
Air China	-200F	1		-400	19		-100B	3
	-200B SCD	3		-400F	5		-200B	10
	-400	6	China Airlines	-200B	1		-200B SCD	2
	-400 SCD	8		-200B SCD	3		-200F	8
Air Djibouti	-200B	1		-200F	2		-300	13
Air France	-200B	1		-400	13		-400	41
	-200B SCD	9		-400F	8	Japan Asia Airways	-200B	3
	-200F	11	Comores Airlines	SP	1		-300	1
	-300 SCD	2	Corsair	-200B	2	Japanese Air Self Defence		
	-400	7		SP	1	Force	-400	2
	-400 SCD	6		-300	4	Kabo Air	-100	4
Air Gabon	-200B SCD	1	Dragonair	-300 SCD	2		-200B	1
Air Gulf Falcon	-200B	2	Dubai Air Wing	-200B SCD	1	Kalitta Air	-100 SCD	2
	SP	1	Dubai Government	SP	2		-200B SCD	1
Air Hong Kong	-200B SCD	3	Egypt Air	-300 SCD	2	KLM Royal Dutch Airlines	-200B	2
Air India	-200B	4	El Al	-200B	3		-200B SCD	7
	-300 SCD	2		-200B SCD	1		-300 SCD	3
	-400	6		-200C	1		-400	6
Air Namibia	-400 SCD	1		-200F	2		-400 SCD	15
Air New Zealand	-400	8		-400	4	Korean Air	-200B	2
Air Pacific	-200B	1	European Aun	-200B	2		-200B SCD	2
Airfreight Express	-200F	2	Eva Airways	-400	7		-200F	5
Alitalia	-200B	7		-400 SCD	7		-300	1
	-200B SCD	1		-400F	1		-300 SCD	1
	-200F	1	Evergreen International				-400	26
All Nippon Airways	SR	11	Airlines	-100 SCD	4		-400 SCD	1
	-200B	3		-200C	2		-400F	8
	-400	23		-200B SCD	3	Kuwait Airways	-200B SCD	1
Asiana Airlines	-400	4		SR SCD	1		-400 SCD	1
	-400 SCD	4	Garuda Indonesian Airways	-200B	4	Lufthansa	-200B	4
	-400F	4		-400	3		-200B SCD	4
Atlas Air	-200C	1	GE Aircraft Engines Inc	-100 SCD	1		-400	23
	-200B SCD	19	Global Supply Systems	-400F	1		-400 SCD	7
	-200F	1	Hydro Air	-200C	1	Lufthansa Cargo	-200F	5
	-300 SCD	2	Iberia	-200B	5		-200B SCD	3
	-400F	9		-200B SCD	2	Malaysian Airline System	-200B SCD	2

Left: Boeing 747-422 N194UA (c/n 26892) displays the latest livery of United Air Lines as it climbs out of Las Vegas McCarran International Airport in October 1999. The airline is currently the second largest -400 series operator after British Airways, with some 44 examples on its books. (Airliner World - Mark Nicholls)

Right: This image must be one of the few of this particular aircraft with this airline. Boeing 747-128 F-BPVD (c/n 19752) was delivered to Air France on July 14, 1970. It was leased to a number of operators during its career including Middle East Airlines, which operated it for just eight days between June 25 and July 2, 1993. It was subsequently bought by AAR Aviation Trading in January 1994 before being retired and used for spares recovery at Oklahoma City in February that year. (Chris Penney)

Right: This 747-236B was originally intended for British Airways, but was not taken up by the UK carrier. Instead it was delivered to Malaysian Airline System as 9M-MHI (c/n 22304) on March 12, 1983. It saw brief leasing periods with Garuda Indonesian Airways and Air New Zealand during 1994 before being converted to a freighter in October 1995. (Airliner World collection)

CURRENT BOEING 747 OPERATORS (continued)								
Operator	**Type**	**Aircraft**	**Operator**	**Type**	**Aircraft**	**Operator**	**Type**	**Aircraft**
	-300 SCD	1		-400	3	Singapore Airlines	-400	38
	-400	15		-400 SCD	1		-400 SCD	1
	-400 SCD	2	Polar Air Cargo	-100 SCD	7		-400F	9
Martinair Holland	-200C	2		200F	4	South African Airways	-200B	5
	-200F	1		-200B SCD	3		SP	3
	-300 SCD	1		-400F	3		-300	6
MK Airlines	-200F	1	Qantas	-200B	2		-400	8
	-200B SCD	1		-200B SCD	2	Southern Air	-200B SCD	3
NASA	SR	1		-300	6	Syrianair	SP	2
	SP	1		-400	25	Taag Angola Airlines	-300 SCD	2
Nigerian Airlines	-200b	1	Qatar Government	SP	1	Thai Airways International	-300	2
Nippon Cargo Airlines	-200F	6	Royal Air Maroc	-200B SCD	1		-400	16
	-200B SCD	3		-400	1	Transjet Airways	-200B	2
	SR SCD	1	Royal Flight of Oman	-400	1	United Air Lines	-200B	1
Northwest Airlines	-200B	21	Saha Airlines	-100 SCD	2		-400	44
	-200B SCD	2		-200F	3	United Parcel Service	-100 SCD	11
	-200F	10	Saudi Arabian Airlines	-100B	7		-200B	1
	-400	14		-200F	1		-200B SCD	7
Oman Government	SP	2		SP	1		SR SCD	1
Orient Thai Aieways	-200B	1		-300	10	United States Air Force	-200B	6
Pakistan International Airlines	-200B	6		-400	5		-400F	1
	-200B SCD	2	Saudi Arabian			Virgin Atlantic Airways	-400	11
	-300	5	Government	SP	2	Yemen Government	SP	1
Philippine Airlines	-200B	3		-300	1	*Data correct to March 2002.*		

Above: This 747-127, CF-DJC (c/n 20208), got off to an uninspiring start, having been destined for a succession of carriers in the early 1970s but not taken up by any of them. Braniff Airways was to have taken the aircraft in 1971, followed by Universal and Wardair Canada. The latter airline finally accepted the aircraft on April 23, 1973. Subsequently, it passed to a number of leasing companies and saw service with numerous carriers before finally being stored at Manston, Kent, in 1998. (Chris Penney)

Centre left: The same aircraft, c/n 20208, this time during a brief leasing period with Nationair in the early 1990s, is seen about to land at Miami International Airport. (Chris Penney)

Left: Australian carrier Qantas has used every version of the 747 except the SR, and was recently confirmed as the launch customer for the new extended range 747-400ER. Here one of its -200s in the older Qantas livery is pushed back prior to another long flight to the Southern Hemisphere in September 1984. (Chris Penney)

Above: Just two years old when this photograph was taken in November 2000, Air New Zealand 747-419 ZK-NBV (c/n 26910) seen about to land at Los Angeles after a long flight across the Pacific. The aircraft is wearing the latest livery of the carrier, which currently flies eight -400 series 747s. (Robbie Shaw)

Right: A Kalitta American International Airways 747-200 Freighter at Kai Tak in 1996. The airline was formed in November 1972 as Connie Kalitta Services and originally confined its operations to North America. It has since merged with other airlines, including Jet Way, Zantop Airlines and MGM Grand Air, and acquired its 747s during the 1990s. (Airliner World – Malcolm English)

Right: Spanish carrier Iberia currently has seven -200 series 747s and three -300 series for use on its long-haul international routes. Most of its aircraft are configured to carry 408 passengers, though one takes 390 and a 200 combi carries 278. This example, 747-267B TF-ABP (c/n 22429) is seen at Madrid in March 2000 and is sub-leased from Air Atlanta Iceland, which leases it from Cathay Pacific. (Airliner World – Chris Penney)

Above: Garuda Indonesian Airways 747-2U3B PK-GSA (c/n 22246) at London Gatwick in October 1985, displaying the airline's old-style livery. (Chris Penney)

Left: Air Atlanta Icelandic was founded in 1986 and concentrates on providing wet-lease aircraft to other airlines in need of extra capacity. Current customers include Iberia, Monarch and Saudia. Illustrated is 747-267B TF-ATC (c/n 22149) at London Gatwick on May 22, 2000, this aircraft having originally been delivered to Cathay Pacific on July 16, 1980. (Robbie Shaw)

Left: Trans World Airlines (TWA) is a name synonymous with long-haul travel, though today it is more usually confined to short-haul routes in the USA and will shortly be absorbed by American Airlines. Boeing 747-206B N306TW stands forlornly at Marana, Arizona, in September 1998, minus its engines. The aircraft was originally delivered to KLM on August 31, 1971, and after a period of lease arrangements was bought by TWA on March 31, 1994. It was sold to Pegasus Capital Corporation in July 1996 and leased back to the airline before entering storage. (Airliner World – Dave Allport)

Above: Until recently Greek carrier Olympic Airways operated two 747-200s on international services from Athens. 747-212B SX-OAE (c/n 21935) comes in to land at Athens in October 1999, its Krüeger leading edge flaps fully extended along with the massive triple slotted trailing edge flaps. It is these advanced hi-lift devices that allow this huge aircraft to land at such modest speeds. (Airliner World – Ken Delve)

Below: B-2450 (c/n 23746), a 747-2J6B combi operated by Air China, which effectively 'borrows' aircraft from the Civil Aviation Administration of China (CAAC) fleet. CAAC took delivery of this aircraft on March 28, 1987, and it has since been converted to a freighter, though it has remained with the operator. (Chris Penney)

Above: Brazilian carrier Varig introduced the 747-300 on its route to London in the 1980s, to replace the DC-10s then in use on the service. Illustrated is 747-341 combi PP-VNH (c/n 23394) in storage at Rio de Janeiro International Airport, minus engine cores, on September 14, 1999. The airline has since disposed of all its 747s, and this aircraft is now registered to Atlas Air as N354MC. (Airliner World – Robbie Shaw)

Left: Royal Jordanian Airlines no longer operates the 747, although it took delivery of three examples. The first was this one, 747-2D3B combi JY-AFA (c/n 21251), which was delivered to the Middle East operator on April 13, 1977. It was subsequently sold to Aeronautics Leasing Inc in February 1989 and was converted to a freighter in November 1992. In recent years it has been leased to Atlas Air and sub-leased to China Airlines. (Chris Penney)

Left: Northwest Airlines currently has ten 747-200F freighters for use on worldwide cargo services. This example is seen on a sunny ramp at Kai Tak in 1996. (Airliner World – Malcolm English)

Above: Aerolineas Argentinas took delivery of this 747-287B, LV-MLP (c/n 21726), on October 11, 1979, and although it was sold to General Electric Capital Aviation Services in June 1996, it was leased back to the airline and remains one of seven examples in use by the Latin American carrier. (Nigel Prevett)

Below: One of the most prolific Asian operators of the Jumbo is Singapore Airlines. Currently 38 of 42 747-412s ordered have been delivered to the airline, including this one, 9V-SMI (c/n 24975), which arrived on February 25, 1991. (Airliner World – Tony Dixon)

Left: Italian carrier Alitalia has a modest fleet of ten 747s, including 747-243B I-DEMV (c/n 23301) captured on film at Rio de Janeiro on September 19, 1999. (Robbie Shaw)

Right: Boeing 747-151 N601US (c/n 19778) was one of a number operated by Northwest Orient Airlines, later Northwest Airlines, on international routes. (Chris Penney)

Centre left: A TWA 747-200 at the end of another transatlantic flight in June 1989, displaying the livery of the period. The aircraft is approaching London Heathrow, but the airline subsequently gave up its Heathrow slots to American Airlines and has now retired its 747s. (Chris Penney)

Right: One of the 57 -400 series Jumbos owned by British Airways, the largest single operator of the latest 747 model. BA 747-436 G-BNLP (c/n 24058) climbs hard out of London Gatwick in April 2000. (Robbie Shaw)

Bottom left: Air Pacific 747-238B VH-EBK (c/n 21140) at Sydney on October 16, 1988. The airline leased the aircraft from Qantas between March 1985 and February 1989. Fiji-based Air Pacific began life as Fiji Airways in 1951 and was renamed in 1971 when the island governments of Fiji, Kiribati, Tonga and Nauru gained a controlling interest in the airline. The carrier operates services in the south-western Pacific to Australia, New Zealand and Japan, as well as to other Pacific islands. (Nigel Prevett)

Right: Thai Airways International now operates a pair of -300 series and 16 -400 series 747s. This 747-2D7B, HS-TGS (c/n 22472) seen landing at Kai Tak in November 1994, was delivered to the Thai operator on June 1, 1984, and stayed with the airline until sold to Atlas Air in June 1997. It was converted to a freighter and leased to China Airlines. (Robbie Shaw)

Top: Cathay Pacific Airways 747-467 VR-HOY (c/n 25351) at Kai Tak in 1996 wearing the older paint scheme. The aircraft was delivered on November 22, 1991, and re-registered as B-HOY in August 1997. (Airliner World – Malcolm English)

Above: A pair of 747-481Ds of All Nippon Airways at Haneda, Japan, on November 19, 1996. Both aircraft were delivered to the airline in 1993 for use on the high-density domestic Japanese routes. The nearest aircraft, JA8961 (c/n 25644) sports distinctive 'Charlie Brown' artwork. (Nigel Prevett)

Left: SIA 747-212B 9V-SQQ (c/n 21942) undergoing maintenance at Singapore Airlines facilities – note the starboard outer engine has been removed. This aircraft was sold to Northwest Airlines in July 1996. (Airliner World – Malcolm English)

Right: The old colour scheme used by United Airlines looks somewhat dated compared with some of the liveries to be seen on the latest airliners. Here 747-122 N4718U (c/n 19879) heads for the gate after another long-haul flight in 1990. This aircraft was eventually used for spares recovery at Ardmore, Oklahoma, in 1998. (Chris Penney)

Centre right: South African Airways 747-244B combi ZS-SAR (c/n 22170) joined the airline on November 6, 1980, and apart from lease to Garuda Indonesian Airlines between 1992 and 1994, it has remained with the African carrier. It was converted to a freighter in 1995 but is seen here in July 1984 wearing the airline's old, and rather attractive, livery. (Chris Penney)

Below: Nigeria Airways continues to operate a single 747: currently this is 747-236B G-BDXB (c/n 21239), under lease from British Airways. The aircraft is seen landing at London Heathrow in May 2000. (Airliner World – Steve Fletcher)

⑬ COCKPITS AND INTERIORS

Anyone who has flown on a 747 finds their most abiding impression is of the vast size of its cabin. In the early 1970s, the seating in all classes was considered luxurious, though today it would be seen as basic. Aircraft interiors have evolved considerably since then, as have seat design, cabin layout and finishing. Today the latest 400 aircraft have built-in video screens for each seat, and the 'Boeing Connexion', to be included shortly, will introduce real-time TV, e-mail and Internet access while airborne. Modern, lightweight, fire-resistant materials now fill the cabin and combined with innovative design features, these create an almost completely new interior compared to that of the earliest 747-100s. Should Boeing decide to resurrect the 747X programme, the advanced and award-winning interior architecture from the 777 family will be used throughout.

The flight deck has also undergone a revolution since it was designed in the mid-1960s. Up to and including the -300 series, all 747s had a three-man flight crew: captain, co-pilot and flight engineer. Instrumentation was typical of the analogue period, with some 971 switches and gauges spread across a number of panels. The advent of the -400 saw a complete re-design of the cockpit and the introduction of the latest technology, including the use of 'glass cockpit' multi-function display screens. Improved navigation equipment was added, along with a massive increase in onboard computer power which enabled a considerable number of checklist items to be automated. This also helped to reduce the number of switches and dials to 365, to eliminate the flight engineer's position, and considerably reduce the pilot workload.

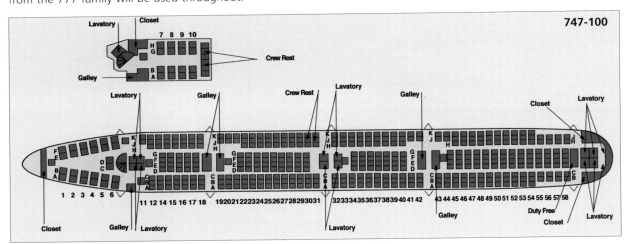

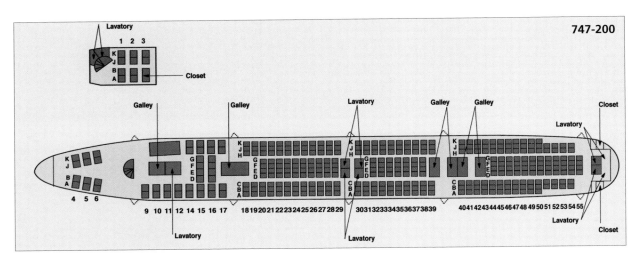

Left: Typical cabin layout of a United Airlines 747-100. (Pete West)

Lower left: Garuda Indonesia cabin layout for its 747-200s, with rows 1-17 configured as Executive Class. (Pete West)

Bottom left: The latest Upper Class seats for Virgin Atlantic Airways are a far cry from those available only ten years ago. (Virgin Atlantic Airways)

Below: The upper deck of the first Singapore Airlines 747-300 *Big Top* provided the airline with increased Business Class space and came complete with its own galley at the rear. (Singapore Airlines)

Right: Swissair 747-357M combi offered the airline the ability to carry a mixed load of passengers and cargo. The airline was the launch customer for the -300 series, though it received only limited orders and was soon superseded by the more advanced -400 with further interior improvements. (Pete West)

747-357 Mixed

Right: The -400 series gave more possibilities for interior layouts than had been afforded by previous models. Illustrated is the latest 747-436 layout for British Airways that includes the large sleeper bed seats in First Class rows 1-5. (Pete West)

747-400

Right: Australian carrier Qantas has used this layout for its 747SP-38s. Note the use of a two-class system, with Business Class in rows 1-5 and 11-13 on the upper deck. (Pete West)

747SP-38

Below: Cross sections showing the various seating widths available in First, Business and Economy Class cabins of the 747. (Pete West)

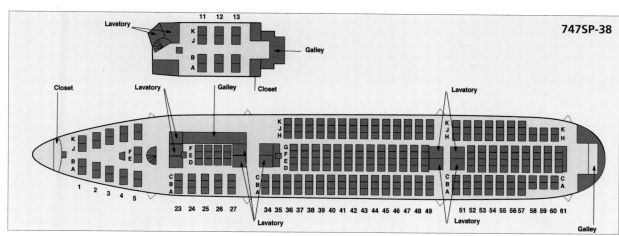

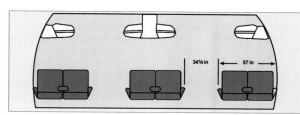

First Class

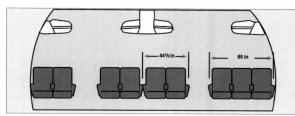

Business Class

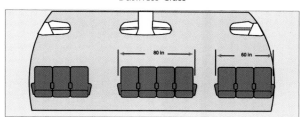

Economy Class

An early 1970s economy interior of a 747-100. Notice the vastness of the cabin, which at the time must have seemed a world apart from the 707s and DC-8s of the period. (Boeing)

Above left: A Lufthansa 747-130 Economy Class interior of 1970. Much has changed aboard the latest 747s, including a considerable increase in the overhead stowage bin size. (Lufthansa)

Above: One of the most attractive features of the early -100 series, and indeed of some -200s, was the spiral staircase connecting the main deck with the upper deck. Latest production 747s have abandoned this feature for a more conventional straight design. (Boeing)

Left: 'Spacious' would be one way to describe the latest First Class cabin on KLM 747s. The facilities and comfort available to First and Business Class passengers is constantly being improved to satisfy the demands of the customer and to compete with rival airlines. (KLM)

Above: The Upper Class bar aboard a Virgin Atlantic Airways 747. The bar was popular in the early 1970s – it was a novel feature when it was introduced on the first 747s. Some airlines dropped it in favour of extra seating, though others still retain the feature. (Virgin Atlantic Airways)

Right: Lufthansa Business Class in 1979, a far cry from that available today. Here the seating is nine across, only one short of Economy Class. Today the majority of airlines offer much wider seats, though the fares often reflect the extra space and facilities afforded to passengers. However, with business travel now contributing a quite substantial sum to many airlines' profits, it is understandable that they are prepared to offer their Business customers the best possible accommodation. (Lufthansa)

Right: The latest upper deck First Class seats available on Lufthansa 747s. The space and facilities provided are vastly superior to those available at the launch of the original 747-100. Today's passengers have their own video screens and a massive choice of films, interactive computer games, audio channels and other facilities. (Lufthansa)

Left: The cockpit on the -400 series features the latest multi-function colour displays and a great deal of automation. This allows for two-crew operation in complete safety. (Jeff Moss)

Left: The 1960s design of the original 747-100 cockpit is well illustrated here by the massive number of dials and gauges. (Boeing)

Below: The Flight Engineer's panel on a Virgin Atlantic Airways 747-200, showing the vast array of instruments. The 747-400 did away with the flight engineer's position completely, modern computer technology taking over many of the tasks while the remainder were simplified and passed over to the captain and co-pilot. (Airliner World – Chris Penney)

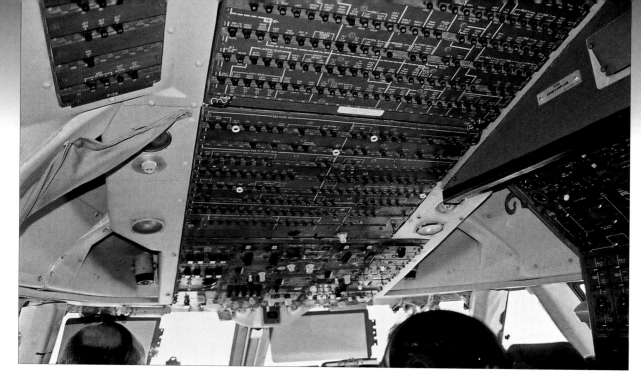

Right: The overhead panel on a 747-200 presented a huge number of switches and circuit breakers: with the arrival of the -400, the crew's workload was greatly simplified. (Airliner World – Chris Penney)

Right: A Virgin Atlantic Airways' 747-200 in the cruise at about 37,000ft (11,277m). The cockpit, with its analogue dials and plethora of switches, seems very outdated in comparison with the latest 'glass cockpit' technology. (Airliner World – Chris Penney)

Below: The face of modern avionics as depicted in this impression of the cockpit for the planned 747X. The crew members are presented with easy-to-read information for the relevant flight profile on the multi-functional display screens. The 747X cockpit is fairly similar to that already available on the 747-400, though it would have included the very latest advances in avionics and new technology. (Boeing)

FUTURE VARIANTS

During the 1990s, Boeing considered a series of developments to the 747-400 known as the -500X and -600X: the latter would have been able to carry up to 700 passengers. Both of these aircraft were primarily aimed at the Asian market, but an economic slump in the region resulted in the project being dropped in early 1997.

However, plans were made for an extended range version of the 747-400 to be known as the -400ER in keeping with similar developments of the 767 and 777 airliners. Australian carrier Qantas placed an order for six aircraft on December 19, 2000, with deliveries due between 2002-06. An increase in length of 4ft 2in (1.27m) and a greater wingspan of 229ft (69.8m), coupled with structural strengthening, will permit the carriage of more fuel and payload with the maximum take-off weight rising to 910,000lb (412,776kg). These improvements will give the aircraft a range of 8,850 miles (14,240km) with a load of around 416 passengers.

The next stage of development was to be the proposed 747X. This aircraft was seen as the ultimate development of the original 747 airframe and would be the largest of the family. Weighing in at a colossal 1,043,900lb (473,500kg) the aircraft was expected to be offered in 747X long-range, combi and freighter versions as well as a stretched variant able to carry up to 504 passengers in a three-class layout. Although many saw the aircraft as a competitor to the recently-launched Airbus A380 'Super Jumbo', Boeing saw it as a much cheaper alternative better able to fit in with current 747 operators' plans and procedures. However, with no launch customer apparently in sight Boeing took the decision in March 2001 to shelve the 747X and instead concentrate on a new breed of airliner capable of flight just below the speed of sound. However, markets do change and so Boeing is keeping its options open, maintaining that it could re-start the 747X program quickly if the airlines show renewed interest. For the moment the company is concentrating its efforts on small improvements to the -400, the extended range version being the current priority following a launch order from Qantas.

Below: The 747X stretch would be the largest 747 if it is built. This version has the capacity to carry over 520 passengers in a three-class layout, but if it was configured for the Japanese domestic market, this figure would increase to well over 600. (Boeing)

Bottom: Artist's impression of the First Class cabin at the front of the proposed 747X. Use of the award-winning 777 interior architecture would provide a bright and pleasant environment. The sleeper seats would be flexible and comfortable to give maximum customer satisfaction on long-haul flights. (Boeing)

747X SPECIFICATIONS	
Wingspan	228ft 11in (69.77m)
Length	241ft 1in (73.47m)
Height	70ft 4in (21.44m)
Wing area	6,800sq ft (632m^2)
Weight empty	391,000lb (177,400kg)
Weight maximum	1,043,000lb (473,100kg)
Fuel capacity	72,573 US gals (274,720 litres)
Cruising speed	Mach 0.86
Ceiling	45,000ft (13,700m)
Range	10,340 miles (16,640km)
Passenger capacity	Up to 442 typically in three classes
Powerplants	choice of
	4 x Engine Alliance GP7168
	4 x Rolls-Royce Trent 600

Right: Among the proposals for the 747X is use of the space above the main deck, including more private 'lounge' areas for First and Business Class passengers. (Boeing)

Below: Cutaway view of the proposed 747X Stretch. (Boeing)

Bottom: At the Asian Aerospace 2002 trade show Boeing announced it was launching the 747-400X QLR (Quiet Longer Range) version of the 747-400. The aircraft could be ready to enter service as early as 2004 depending on customer demand. As well as offering increased range the aircraft will be noticeably quieter on approach (40%) and take-off (20%) and will also offer better fuel efficiency with reduced emissions. (Boeing)

LOSSES

The safety record of the 747 is one of the most remarkable in aviation history. Over 1,200 aircraft have been built and in the millions of hours and millions of miles they have flown, only three have been lost to what appear to be design faults or structural failures. All others have been through other means, such as terrorism or human error. The last of the three which fell victim to technical failures was the TWA 747-131 lost on July 17, 1996, due to fuel vapour ignition in the centre fuselage fuel tank, shortly after departure from New York.

The other two were freighters which lost engines from the wing just after take-off, one in Taiwan on December 29, 1991, and one in Amsterdam on October 4, 1992. Investigations put the blame on corroded pylon attachment pins, of which there were four for each engine, and Boeing instigated a replacement programme which also saw the fitting of two extra corrosion-resistant steel mountings. The cost per aircraft was $1 million and was split between Boeing and the airlines. As well as modifying all existing aircraft, the new procedure was incorporated on the 747-400 production line.

In all other circumstances, the aircraft itself can in no way be blamed for its loss – quite an amazing feat for a design dating back 30 years or more which still sees such intense service.

Top left: Air India's 747-237B VT-EFO (c/n 21473) was delivered to the airline on June 30, 1978. This aircraft was lost when a terrorist bomb exploded over the Atlantic Ocean, west of Ireland, on June 23, 1985. (Boeing)

Second left: Cameroon Airlines 747-2H7B TJ-CAB (c/n 22378) is the only 747 to be owned by the carrier and was delivered new on February 26, 1982. It overran the runway at Paris Charles de Gaulle Airport, France, on November 5, 2000, and was damaged beyond repair. (Robbie Shaw)

Third left: One of the two 747s lost in the early 1990s due to engine separation was this aircraft, c/n 22390, seen here in 1985 during a lease period with Cargolux. The operator actually took delivery of this 747-2R7F as new in October 1980 and subsequently sold it to China Airlines in February 1985. Cargolux then leased it back for four months before returning it to the Asian operator. The aircraft crashed shortly after departure from Taipei, Taiwan, on December 29, 1991, when the number three engine separated from the wing. (Chris Penney)

Bottom: The charred remains of British Airways 747-136 G-AWND (c/n 19764), destroyed by shellfire at Kuwait International Airport on February 27, 1991, during the Gulf War. (Airliner World – Duncan Cubitt)

Date	Reg	Type	Carrier	Fate
6 Sept 70	N752PA	747-121	Pan Am	Destroyed by terrorists, Cairo, Egypt, after hijack.
24 July 73	JA8109	747-246B	JAL	Destroyed by terrorists, Benghazi, Libya, after hijack.
20 Nov 74	D-ABYB	747-130	Lufthansa	Failure to deploy leading edge flaps on departure from Nairobi, Kenya.
12 June75	F-BPVJ	747-128	Air France	Destroyed by fire, Bombay, India.
27 March 77	N736PA	747-121	Pan Am	Collision in fog at Los Rodeos, Tenerife, Canary Islands.
	PH-BUF	747-206B	KLM	Collision in fog at Los Rodeos, Tenerife, Canary Islands.
1 Jan 78	VT-EBD	747-237B	Air India	Crashed into sea off Bombay, after ADI failure.
19 Nov 80	HL7445	747-2B5B	Korean Air	Landed 300ft (90m) short of runway in fog at Seoul, RoK.
31 Aug 83	HL7442	747-230B	Korean Air	Shot down, Sakhalin, Sea of Japan, by Soviet Su-15.
27 Nov 83	HK-2910	747-283M	AVIANCA	Inaccurate approach near Madrid, Spain.
16 March 85	F-GDUT	747-283	UTA	Fire, Paris Charles de Gaulle, France.
23 June 85	VT-EFO	747-237B	Air India	Destroyed by terrorist bomb west of Ireland.
12 Aug 85	JA8119	747-SR-46	JAL	Crashed into Mount Osutako, Japan, following aft pressure bulkhead failure caused by improper repair.
2 Dec 85	F-GCBC	747-228M	Air France	Ran off runway at Rio-Galeao, Brazil.
28 Nov 87	ZS-SAS	747-244M	SAA	Intense fire developed in cargo hold, crashed into Indian Ocean.
21 Dec 88	N739PA	747-121	PanAm	Destroyed by terrorist bomb over Lockerbie, Scotland.
19 Feb 89	N807FT	747-249F	Flying Tigers	Flew into ground, Punchong, Malaysia.
7 April 90	VT-EBO	747-237B	Air India	Destroyed by fire, New Delhi, India.
2 Aug 90	G-AWND	747-136	BA	Destroyed by shelling, Kuwait International Airport.
29 Dec 91	B-198V	747-2R7F	China Airlines	Number three engine separated from wing after take-off from Taipei, Taiwan.
4 Oct 92	4X-AXG	747-258F	El Al	Number three engine separated from wing, crashed into apartment block in Bijlmermeer, Amsterdam, The Netherlands.
12 Sept 93	F-GITA	747-428	Air France	Veered off runway at Papeete.
4 Nov 93	B-165	409	China Airlines	Overran runway, Hong Kong, Kai Tak. Instructional airframe.
20 Dec 95	N605FF	747-136	Tower Air	Aborted take-off at New York JFK.
17 July 96	N93119	747-131	TWA	Crashed into Atlantic off Long Island, NY, due to fuel-tank explosion.
12 Nov 96	HZ-AIH	747-168B	Saudi Arabian	Mid-air collision with Il-76 UN-75435 of Kazakhstan Airlines over Charkhi Dadri, India.
6 Sept 97	HL7468	747-385	Korean Air	Crashed into high ground on approach to Agana, Guam.
6 March 99	F-GPAN	747-2B3F	Air France	Destroyed by fire, Madras-Chennah Airport, India.
22 Dec 99	HL7451	747-2B5F	Korean Air	Crashed after take-off from London Stansted Airport.
31 Oct 00	9V-SPK	747-412	Singapore Airlines	Collided with machinery while attempting to depart from closed runway at Taipei/Chiang Kai-Shek International Airport, Taiwan.
5 Nov 00	TJ-CAB	747-2H7B	Cameroon Airlines	Damaged beyond repair after over-running the runway on landing at Paris Charles de Gaulle Airport.
25 May 02	B-18255	747-209B	China Airlines	Disappeared from radar while en-route from Taipei to Hong Kong

Right: The second 747 lost due to engine separation was 747-258F 4X-AXG (c/n 21737) which crashed into an apartment block at Bijlmermeer, Amsterdam, on October 4, 1992. The aircraft is seen here at London Heathrow in May 1986 wearing the El Al scheme of the period, but no titles other than 'cargo'. Terminal 4 can be seen under construction in the background. (Chris Penney)

Right: Former Air France 747-128 F-BPVE was used in an experiment on May 17, 1997, to help design luggage containers more able to withstand the effects of bomb explosions. The untreated container had this effect when detonated, a modified one in the forward hold contained the explosion without damage to the aircraft's structure or skin. (Airliner World - Dave Allport)

The size of the 747 is clearly illustrated by this South African Airways example as it dwarfs the ground support equipment. (Airline World – Tony Dixon)